American Come Back

The Fusion of AI and Hydrogen

Thomas Anastasiadis

Contents

Dedication

In the poetic embrace of dedication, I humbly offer this book to my dearest wife. A tribute to the resilience etched in every line of her journey, a testament to the enduring strength she possesses. May these pages reflect the depth of gratitude for her unwavering, everlasting love that has illuminated the path of my existence.

Acknowledgment

In the quiet corners of existence, I extend heartfelt acknowledgments to life itself—a profound architect, sculpting me through the crucible of difficulties, the echoes of suffering, and the intricate dance of struggles. Each trial etched a line in the narrative, forging the unique story that is me. With gratitude, I embrace the lessons woven into the tapestry of my being, a poetic acknowledgment to the symphony of life's challenges that contributed to the creation of the person I am today.

About the Author

Introducing our author, a true testament to the transformative power of passion and resilience. Born into adversity, raised in the unforgiving embrace of a ghetto, our author defied the odds in a journey that steered clear of traditional paths. Uneducated and without the formal trappings of official degrees, life took an unexpected turn, entwining him with the shadows of organized crime.

However, within the confines of prison walls, a metamorphosis occurred. Stripped of conventional education, the author discovered an insatiable hunger for knowledge, a flame that burned brighter with each passing day. For four years straight, he delved into the realms of philosophy, science, artificial intelligence, and history, voraciously consuming literature from the break of dawn until the nightfall. Each waking moment became an opportunity to unravel the mysteries of the world through the pages that unfolded before him.

This was no indulgence in escapist fantasies or romantic tales. No, the author sought intellectual sustenance, immersing himself in subjects that explored the depths of human existence. Emerging from the crucible of incarceration, he emerged not as a former prisoner, but as a reborn individual with an ignited passion for the written word.

The culmination of this profound journey is the book before you. It delves into the annals of the past, navigates the complexities of the present, and casts a hopeful gaze towards an even more promising future. Born from the crucible of human experience, this work reflects a deep understanding of the human condition and the aspirations that unite us.

With a heart fueled by a special love for freedom, equality, and the development of individuals, our author envisions a world shaped by the principles of a liberal country like America. Through the art of storytelling, he weaves a narrative that transcends boundaries, inviting readers to contemplate the essence of humanity and the possibilities that lie ahead.

Join us on this remarkable literary journey, as we celebrate an author whose life story is as captivating as the words he pens—a testament to the boundless potential within every soul, waiting to be unearthed and shared with the world.

Preface

Harmony in Innovation

In the quiet spaces between pixels and hydrogen atoms, where technology and human dreams converge, lies a vision of renewal for a nation dear to the heart. As the quill of progress inscribes its lines on the parchment of time, this book, born of admiration and love, seeks to gently stir the winds of change.

In the mosaic of human existence, the author, though not a resident, feels an undeniable kinship with the land called the United States of America. It is a place where the echoes of innovation resonate through the canyons of history, and the dance of diversity paints a portrait of boundless potential.

The pages within unfold a narrative that looks beyond the shadows of current divisions. In a world where artificial intelligence and fuel cells emerge as silent architects of tomorrow, the author envisions a symphony of harmony in innovation. It is a call to every American, regardless of their journey or background, to join hands in steering the ship of progress toward calmer, more united waters.

As racial and partisan tempests brew, this book stands as a quiet lighthouse, gently illuminating the shores of possibility. It whispers that in the embrace of technology, every American has the power to redefine the narrative, to bridge the gaps, and to sow the seeds of a flourishing future.

So, let these words be a soft murmur in the reader's ears—a poetic invitation to explore the limitless potential within and around, to dream of an America where the symphony of innovation harmonizes with the soulful heartbeat of its citizens. In this tale of wires and whispers, may the journey commence, and may the vision of a revitalized nation find a home in every heart that turns these pages.

Chapter 1
Pioneers and Pilgrims

The Dawn of European Settlement in America

In the early 16th century, a wave of exploration and expansion swept across the Atlantic as European powers sought new lands and opportunities. The first Europeans to leave an indelible mark on what would become the United States were the Spanish conquistadors. In 1565, led by the determined Pedro Menéndez de Avilés, the Spanish established St. Augustine in the lush landscapes of Florida. This coastal settlement marked the inception of a new era and is recognized as the oldest continuously inhabited European-established town in the continental United States.

As the Spanish ventured further into the Southeast, English eyes turned westward in search of riches and a route to the Pacific. In 1607, the Virginia Company planted the seeds of English colonization with the establishment of Jamestown in Virginia. This venture faced numerous challenges, including disease, famine, and conflicts with indigenous populations. Despite these hardships, Jamestown persevered and became a crucial player in the shaping of America.

Meanwhile, a group of Pilgrims, seeking religious freedom, embarked on a perilous journey across the Atlantic. The Mayflower landed at Plymouth in 1620, where these pioneers laid the foundations for the

Plymouth Colony. Their encounter with the Wampanoag Native Americans culminated in the first Thanksgiving in 1621, an event that would echo through the ages.

The Dutch also left their mark on the American landscape, establishing New Amsterdam on the southern tip of Manhattan Island in 1624. This outpost, a melting pot of diverse cultures, would later transform into the bustling metropolis of New York City.

As the French ventured into North America, Samuel de Champlain founded Quebec in 1608, marking the beginning of French influence in the region.

Through these early settlements, the stage was set for centuries of European exploration, competition, and the complex interactions with the indigenous peoples who had called this land home for millennia. The chapters that follow will unfold the tapestry of America's history - a story of resilience, conflict, and the pursuit of a new identity.

Shadows of Conquest - The Painful Legacy

In recounting the early European settlement, it is essential to confront the shadows that loom over this historical tapestry. The arrival of European conquerors was not merely a peaceful coexistence of different worlds; it was a brutal invasion, marked by violence, theft, and the enslavement of the native population.

As the Spanish, English, Dutch, and French staked their claims, the indigenous peoples faced not only the diseases brought by the newcomers but also a wave of violence that would reshape their societies. Entire civilizations crumbled, languages were lost, and sacred lands were seized.

Jamestown, while celebrated as a bastion of English colonization, was also witness to the dispossession of Native Americans from their ancestral lands. The narrative of cooperation during the first Thanksgiving in Plymouth is juxtaposed with the tragedies that followed - the forced removals, broken treaties, and the erosion of indigenous cultures.

The Dutch, seeking economic prosperity in New Amsterdam, participated in the global slave trade, bringing untold suffering to countless individuals who were forcibly displaced from their homelands and forced into bondage.

As we delve into the annals of history, it is imperative to strip away the romanticized notions and confront the painful truths. The descendants of those who suffered the gravest injustices continue to grapple with the repercussions of this history today. Understanding this legacy is not an act of blame but a call to acknowledge the interconnectedness of our shared past.

In the chapters that follow, we will explore the ongoing journey of America, a nation built on the resilience of diverse peoples. It is through this unflinching examination of our history that we pave the way for a future founded on justice, understanding, and a collective commitment to a more inclusive narrative.

Chapter 2

From Diverse Horizons

The Tapestry of Modern America

As we traverse the currents of time from the early European settlement to the present-day United States of America, the story unfolds as a magnificent tapestry woven with threads from every corner of the globe. The magic of this narrative lies in the diversity of voices, cultures, and dreams that have converged to shape the modern mosaic of America.

In the crucible of history, waves of immigrants embarked on arduous journeys, seeking refuge, opportunity, and a chance to contribute to the ever-evolving narrative. The 19th and early 20th centuries witnessed the arrival of millions from Europe, Asia, and beyond, drawn by the promise of the American Dream. The stories of Ellis Island, Angel Island, and the bustling streets of cities like New York and San Francisco echo with the resilience of those who dared to dream.

The struggles and triumphs of African Americans, who endured the horrors of slavery and later fought for civil rights, are integral to this saga. Their cultural contributions, from music to literature, have left an indelible mark, enriching the very soul of the nation.

The mid-20th century brought seismic shifts with the Civil Rights Movement, women's liberation, and the fight for LGBTQ+ rights. The struggle for equality became a rallying cry, inspiring movements that continue to shape the trajectory of the nation.

The latter part of the 20th century saw the influx of immigrants from Latin America, the Middle East, and Africa, contributing to the vibrant tapestry of cultures that now defines America. The celebration of diversity became a national strength, fostering innovation, creativity, and a shared commitment to progress.

In the 21st century, the digital revolution has interconnected the world in ways unimaginable to those early pioneers. The power of information, the rise of social movements, and the collective efforts to address global challenges highlight the interconnectedness of humanity.

Yet, challenges persist. The echoes of historical injustices reverberate in contemporary conversations about race, inequality, and justice. The journey towards a more perfect union continues, guided by the ideals set forth by the nation's founders.

As we gaze upon the horizon of today's United States of America, let us recognize the magic embedded in this ever-evolving story. It is a tale of resilience, diversity, and the perpetual pursuit of a more inclusive and equitable society. In understanding our past and embracing our shared future, we find the true enchantment of America.

Chapter 3

Currency of Dreams

The Role of Money in America's Ascent

In the grand narrative of the American empire, the story of money serves as a powerful undercurrent, shaping the course of history and drawing aspirants from every corner of the globe. The allure of prosperity, opportunity, and the pursuit of dreams has been intricately woven into the fabric of the nation, transforming the landscape and beckoning countless individuals to its shores.

The early economic foundations were laid by the enterprising spirit of the colonies, fueled by trade, agriculture, and the pursuit of wealth. As the nation expanded, so did its economic ambitions, culminating in the transformational events of the 20th century.

The aftermath of World War II witnessed the rise of the United States as a global economic powerhouse. The international monetary landscape underwent a paradigm shift with the establishment of the Bretton Woods system, where nations pegged their currencies to the U.S. dollar, and the dollar, in turn, was pegged to gold. This arrangement, along with the creation of the International Monetary Fund (IMF), set the stage for a new era of economic interconnectedness.

The bold and visionary decision to make the U.S. dollar a fiat currency in 1971, severing its ties to gold, marked a pivotal moment in monetary history. This move, orchestrated by President Richard Nixon, unleashed the potential for unprecedented economic growth. The dollar, backed by the strength of the American economy, became a symbol of stability and a universally accepted medium of exchange.

As the dollar assumed its role as the world's primary reserve currency, it played a crucial part in attracting immigrants and foreign investment. The promise of a stable and prosperous economic environment, coupled with the resilience of the American spirit, became a beacon for those seeking a better life.

In the late 20th and early 21st centuries, the digital revolution brought forth a new frontier in the world of finance. The advent of technology transformed the way money was transacted, invested, and accessed, further propelling the American economy into the global spotlight.

As we explore the pages of this monetary saga, it becomes evident that the story of America is not just one of economic triumphs but also of challenges and disparities. The pursuit of economic justice, equitable opportunities, and the continued evolution of the financial landscape remain central to the ongoing narrative of the American empire.

Chapter 4
Shores of Ambition

Immigrants and the Currency of Hope

Against the backdrop of economic aspirations, the shores of America have witnessed waves of immigrants seeking refuge from hardship and chasing the promise of prosperity. The story of money, intertwined with the American dream, became a magnetic force, drawing individuals from diverse backgrounds, each carrying their dreams, skills, and ambitions.

The 19th century saw waves of European immigrants, lured by the prospect of economic opportunity and a chance to redefine their destinies. Ellis Island, standing as a gateway to the American dream, welcomed millions who sought a new beginning.

The economic hardships of the early 20th century, coupled with the promise of employment and a better life, drew immigrants from Asia and Latin America. The currency of hope became a driving force, propelling families across oceans and borders.

The international monetary landscape, shaped by institutions like the IMF and the strategic decision to make the U.S. dollar a fiat currency, played a role in projecting economic stability. This global recognition of the dollar's strength contributed to the nation's appeal, fostering an environment where dreams could be nurtured and ambitions could be realized.

In the contemporary era, as the digital economy reshapes the nature of work and finance, the allure of America persists. Immigrants continue to arrive, not just seeking economic opportunities but also contributing to the rich tapestry of cultures that defines the nation.

As we delve into the human side of this narrative, it becomes clear that the story of money is not just about economic transactions but about the currency of hope, resilience, and the pursuit of a better life. The dreams that echo through the generations of immigrants have become an integral part of the American identity.

Chapter 5

The Alchemy of Innovation

Drawing the Best and Brightest

In the alchemy of innovation, money emerged as a catalyst, drawing the best minds from around the world to contribute their talents and expertise to the ever-expanding canvas of the American story. The allure of a dynamic economy, coupled with the promise of financial backing for groundbreaking endeavors, transformed the United States into a magnet for scientists, researchers, and visionaries.

The 20th century witnessed a scientific and technological renaissance, fueled in part by the economic infrastructure that provided robust funding for research and development. Pioneering minds, from Albert Einstein to countless others, found themselves drawn to the intellectual hub of America, where innovation was not just encouraged but financially supported.

The establishment of research institutions, universities, and corporations that poured resources into scientific endeavors created an ecosystem where ideas flourished. The collaboration between academia, industry, and government, often fueled by substantial financial investments, propelled the United States to the forefront of scientific achievement.

Post-World War II, the landscape of scientific research underwent a transformative phase. The influx of funds, driven by the nation's commitment to technological superiority, resulted in landmark achievements - from the space race to medical breakthroughs.

The establishment of Silicon Valley in the latter half of the 20th century became emblematic of the intersection between money and innovation. Venture capital, angel investors, and a culture that celebrated risk-taking provided fertile ground for entrepreneurs and visionaries. The result was an explosion of technological advancements that reshaped the way humanity lives, works, and communicates.

The financial backing provided by the nation's economic engine not only attracted the best minds but also nurtured a culture that embraced experimentation, creativity, and the pursuit of the unknown. It became a place where scientific breakthroughs were not just celebrated but were seen as integral to the national identity.

As we traverse the landscapes of discovery, it becomes clear that money, as a driving force, played a pivotal role in creating an environment where the best in the field were not only welcomed but were given the resources to push the boundaries of human knowledge.

Chapter 6

Beyond Borders

Global Talent and the Currency of Excellence

The story of money in the context of attracting the best and brightest is not confined by borders. The international appeal of the United States as a hub for excellence in various fields drew talent from every corner of the globe.

The lure of top-tier universities, well-funded research institutions, and a dynamic economy became a beacon for scholars, scientists, and professionals seeking an environment where their skills could flourish. The American dream, intricately linked with the promise of economic prosperity, drew individuals who sought to make an impact and carve out their own path.

In the latter part of the 20th century and into the 21st century, a globalized world saw the United States as a destination for those seeking not just financial success but also the opportunity to collaborate with the best minds in their respective fields. The currency of excellence became a universal language, transcending national boundaries.

Initiatives like the H-1B visa program underscored the nation's recognition of the value that international talent brought to the table. The exchange of ideas, the fusion of diverse perspectives, and the collaborative spirit that emerged became defining elements of America's global influence.

The financial investments in education, research, and technology further solidified the United States as a magnet for global talent. Whether in the realms of science, business, or the arts, the promise of a platform where dreams could be realized drew individuals who sought to contribute to the ongoing narrative of innovation and progress.

As we explore the global dimensions of this narrative, it becomes evident that the story of money is not just about accumulation but about creating a landscape where excellence knows no borders. The best and brightest from around the world became integral threads in the rich tapestry of American achievement.

Chapter 7

Shadows of Wealth

The Dark Side of Economic Power

As we delve deeper into the narrative of money and its role in the American empire, it is essential to acknowledge the shadows that lurk beneath the surface. The lust for wealth, avarice, and the pursuit of economic dominance have cast a complex and often troubling legacy across the pages of history.

The industrialization era of the late 19th and early 20th centuries witnessed the rise of powerful corporations, their fortunes built on the toil of laborers and the ruthless exploitation of resources. The pursuit of profit, at times, led to unethical business practices, monopolies, and the unchecked power of a few individuals who controlled vast economic empires.

Chapter 8

Alchemy of Unity

The Unique Tapestry of America

Amidst the shadows of wealth and the complexities of economic power, a unique alchemy has been unfolding within the United States of America. This nation, often referred to as a "melting pot" or a "salad bowl," has become a crucible of cultures and ideas, fostering a magical tapestry of humanity's development unlike anything witnessed in history.

The United States, from its inception, was envisaged as a land of opportunity, where diverse voices could harmonize in pursuit of shared dreams. Waves of immigrants, driven by the promise of a better life, brought with them the richness of their cultures, traditions, and aspirations.

In the cultural alchemy of America, traditions from Europe, Asia, Africa, and Latin America intermingle, giving birth to a unique and constantly evolving identity. Jazz, born from the African-American experience, reverberates through the streets of New Orleans; the aroma of diverse cuisines wafts from city corners, and the languages spoken reflect a mosaic of global voices.

The Civil Rights Movement, a powerful catalyst for change, ushered in an era of acknowledgment and celebration of diversity. It became a pivotal moment in the nation's history, signaling a commitment to dismantling racial barriers and fostering an environment where every individual, regardless of background, could contribute to the nation's unfolding story.

The 21st century has seen the blossoming of a digital era that connects people across the globe. Social media platforms, created within the borders of America, have become arenas for the exchange of ideas, a virtual melting pot where cultures, opinions, and innovations are shared instantaneously.

The concept of the American Dream, while rooted in the pursuit of economic success, has evolved into something more profound. It embodies the idea that every individual, regardless of their origins, has the potential to contribute to the ongoing narrative of progress and inclusion.

In the alchemy of unity, the United States stands as a testament to the human capacity for transformation. The unique blend of cultures, the resilience of communities, and the shared commitment to liberty and justice have set the stage for a societal experiment unrivaled in history.

Chapter 9
The Collective Symphony

America's Uncharted Journey

As we navigate through the uncharted realms of America's unique journey, the narrative unfolds like a collective symphony, with each individual contributing a distinct note to the composition of humanity's development.

The resilience of the nation, evident in moments of triumph and challenge, mirrors the infinite possibilities that arise when diverse minds come together. It is a testament to the alchemical process of forging a nation, where the heat of shared aspirations transforms the raw materials of individual stories into the golden tapestry of a united society.

In this symphony, the pursuit of knowledge has played a pivotal role. America's universities and research institutions, often at the forefront of global innovation, have become crucibles of ideas that transcend borders. The exchange of knowledge, facilitated by the openness of the American spirit, has propelled humanity forward in unprecedented ways.

The ongoing narrative of America is one of constant evolution, a journey into uncharted territories where the alchemy of unity transforms challenges into opportunities. It is a story that echoes the possibilities inherent in a society that values the contributions of each individual, regardless of their background or origin.

In the chapters that follow, we will explore the uncharted frontiers of the American experiment, examining the complexities, triumphs, and ongoing quest for a society that embraces the full spectrum of human potential. The alchemy of America is a living, breathing testament to the boundless potential of humanity.

Organized crime, epitomized by the likes of the Mafia, infiltrated various sectors, leveraging economic power for illicit gains. From bootlegging during Prohibition to involvement in labor unions and industries, the impact of criminal enterprises left a stain on the nation's moral fabric.

Wars, both overt and covert, waged by companies for control over resources and markets, left scars on the geopolitical landscape. The quest for economic dominance drove conflicts that extended beyond national borders, resulting in environmental degradation and lasting consequences for affected regions.

The hunt for treasure often took a toll on the environment. From the gold rush that scarred landscapes to the industrial pollution that fouled rivers and skies, the pursuit of wealth exacted a heavy toll on the natural world. The consequences of unchecked industrialization and the race for resources reverberate through the decades, manifesting in climate change, deforestation, and the loss of biodiversity.

The military-industrial complex, closely tied to economic interests, played a role in decisions to engage in conflicts, leading to environmental devastation in war-torn regions. The environmental cost of warfare, from the use of Agent Orange in Vietnam to the oil fires of the Gulf War, illustrates the interconnectedness of economic and environmental issues.

Chapter 10

The American Dream

An Unfolding Tapestry

The American Dream, a concept deeply embedded in the fabric of the United States, transcends mere material prosperity. It is a dynamic, ever-evolving notion that encapsulates the aspirations, hopes, and ideals of individuals striving for a better life. At its core, the American Dream encompasses several key elements:

1. Opportunity and Prosperity:

Economic Mobility: The American Dream is synonymous with the belief that hard work, determination, and ingenuity can elevate individuals from any background to economic success.

Prosperity for All: It envisions a society where economic opportunities are widespread, allowing every citizen to achieve financial well-being.

2. Individual Freedom:

Personal Liberty: The American Dream underscores the importance of personal freedom, enabling individuals to pursue their goals, make choices, and carve out their destinies.

Self-Determination: It champions the idea that each person has the autonomy to determine their own path, unencumbered by rigid societal structures.

3. Equality and Justice:

Social Equality: Rooted in the ideals of equality, the American Dream envisions a society where every person has an equal chance to succeed, irrespective of their background.

Fair Justice System: It strives for a legal framework that ensures fairness, justice, and protection of individual rights for all citizens.

4. Homeownership and Stability:

Owning a Home: The dream often includes the aspiration of homeownership, symbolizing stability, security, and a sense of belonging.

Family Well-Being: The American Dream extends to fostering stable families and communities, where individuals can thrive and support one another.

5. Education and Social Mobility:

Educational Attainment: Central to the dream is the belief in the transformative power of education, offering a pathway for upward social mobility.

Meritocracy: It promotes the idea that success is achieved through merit, irrespective of social background or inherited privilege.

6. Pursuit of Happiness:

Personal Fulfillment: Beyond material success, the American Dream encourages the pursuit of happiness in various forms, including personal growth, fulfillment, and meaningful connections.

Cultural Richness: It celebrates the diversity of cultures, ideas, and perspectives that contribute to the nation's vibrant tapestry.

While the American Dream has been a driving force for progress and resilience, it is essential to acknowledge that its realization has been varied and, at times, elusive for different segments of the population. The ongoing dialogue about the American Dream reflects a collective endeavor to continually redefine and expand opportunities for all, ensuring that the dream remains a beacon of aspiration for generations to come.

Chapter 11
The Genesis of Empires

Patterns of Ascent

In the annals of history, empires have risen and fallen, each leaving an indelible mark on the tapestry of human civilization. While the specifics of their stories vary, a closer examination reveals intriguing patterns that echo across time and geography. From the ancient empires of China to the maritime might of the British, certain commonalities emerge in the genesis and ascent of empires.

1. Founding Vision: At the heart of every empire is a founding vision that propels it into existence. Whether rooted in conquest, trade, or cultural dominance, empires often begin with a clear and ambitious vision articulated by visionary leaders. This vision becomes the guiding force, shaping the empire's trajectory from its inception.

2. Expansionary Phase: Empires share a propensity for expansion, driven by factors such as the pursuit of resources, trade routes, or strategic advantages. The early phases are characterized by territorial acquisitions, military conquests, and the establishment of colonies or outposts to extend influence.

3. Economic Foundations: A robust economic foundation is a common thread among successful empires. Whether through control of trade routes, exploitation of natural resources, or the development of advanced economic systems, empires thrive when their economic engines are well-oiled. The accumulation of wealth often becomes a hallmark of their ascendancy.

4. Cultural Hegemony: Cultural influence plays a pivotal role in the ascent of empires. The dissemination of language, art, philosophy, and institutions contributes to cultural hegemony, creating a soft power that extends the empire's reach. The ability to assimilate and incorporate diverse cultures is a key strength during this phase.

5. Military Prowess: Military strength is a recurring theme in the rise of empires. Whether through technological superiority, strategic brilliance, or sheer military might, empires establish dominance on the world stage by securing and defending their interests. The success of military campaigns often becomes a defining factor in their ascent.

6. Institutional Foundations: The establishment of robust institutions is crucial for the longevity of empires. These institutions govern various aspects of society, from administration and justice to education and infrastructure. The stability provided by strong institutions contributes to the empire's resilience in the face of internal and external challenges.

7. Adaptability and Innovation: Successful empires demonstrate a capacity for adaptability and innovation. The ability to evolve with

changing circumstances, embrace new technologies, and navigate geopolitical shifts ensures their continued relevance. Rigidity and resistance to change, on the other hand, can lead to decline.

8. Global Engagement: Empires often reach their zenith when they engage with the broader world. Whether through exploration, trade networks, or diplomatic ties, global engagement enhances their influence. The establishment of a global footprint solidifies their status as major players on the world stage.

As we explore the historical trajectory of empires, it becomes evident that while each empire is unique, the patterns of their ascent share remarkable similarities.

Chapter 12
The Zenith of Empire

At the pinnacle of its glory, an empire radiates a unique brilliance, marked by unprecedented achievements across various facets of its existence. Let us delve into the distinctive characteristics that define an empire at the zenith of its power:

1. Economic Prosperity:

Flourishing Trade: The empire's economic engine hums with the symphony of bustling trade routes, both domestic and international.

Innovation and Entrepreneurship: A surge in innovation and entrepreneurship leads to economic breakthroughs, creating a vibrant marketplace.

2. Artistic Renaissance:

Cultural Flourish: The arts experience a golden age, with prolific creators pushing the boundaries of expression in literature, music, painting, and architecture.

Intellectual Vibrancy: A blossoming of intellectual pursuits fosters an environment where creativity and critical thinking thrive.

3. Military Dominance:

Unmatched Military Prowess: The empire boasts a formidable military, often with cutting-edge technology and superior strategic prowess.

Global Influence: Military victories and strategic alliances extend the empire's influence across borders, projecting power on the world stage.

4. Educational Advancements:

Centers of Learning: Renowned centers of education become beacons of knowledge, attracting scholars and students from far and wide.

Technological Advancements: The empire leads in scientific discoveries and technological advancements, contributing to global progress.

5. Social Harmony:

Inclusive Society: The empire fosters social cohesion, embracing diversity and promoting inclusivity.

Prosperity for Citizens: A majority of citizens experience an improved quality of life, with access to education, healthcare, and ample opportunities.

6. Architectural Marvels:

Grand Infrastructure: Architectural wonders adorn the empire, reflecting the magnificence of its achievements in engineering and design.

Urban Development: Cities thrive with well-planned infrastructure, public spaces, and majestic landmarks.

7. Global Diplomacy:

Diplomatic Influence: The empire's diplomats skillfully navigate international relations, forging alliances and maintaining diplomatic leverage.

Soft Power: Cultural diplomacy and the export of ideas enhance the empire's soft power, fostering positive perceptions globally.

In summary, the zenith of an empire is characterized by a harmonious blend of economic prosperity, artistic brilliance, military might, educational excellence, social cohesion, architectural splendor, and diplomatic finesse. It is a time when the empire stands as a beacon of inspiration, leaving an indelible mark on the pages of history.

Chapter 13
The Ebb of Empires

Factors of Decline

As empires ascend, they also carry within them the seeds of their own decline. The trajectory of empire building is often marked by a rise to power, a period of flourishing dominance, and inevitably, a descent. Examining the factors contributing to the decline of empires reveals recurring patterns that transcend time and geographical boundaries.

1. Economic Strain: Economic factors play a pivotal role in the decline of empires. The overextension of resources, unsustainable economic practices, and a failure to adapt to changing economic landscapes can lead to financial strain. Debt, inflation, and a shrinking tax base are often precursors to economic decline.

2. Military Overreach: While military prowess contributes to the rise of empires, an overreach in military endeavors can lead to their downfall. Extended military campaigns, overdependence on military solutions, and the financial burden of maintaining a vast military apparatus can strain an empire's resources.

3. Internal Dissent and Division: Internal discord and division can erode the stability of empires. Social unrest, ethnic or cultural tensions, and

economic inequality can sow the seeds of discontent. A failure to address internal issues can lead to rebellion, civil wars, or separatist movements, weakening the empire from within.

4. Administrative Corruption and Inefficiency: Corruption and inefficiency within administrative structures can undermine the effectiveness of an empire. A lack of accountability, nepotism, and bureaucratic red tape can hinder governance, leading to a loss of public trust and confidence in the empire's institutions.

5. Technological Stagnation: Technological innovation is a driving force in empire building. Conversely, technological stagnation or a failure to adapt to emerging technologies can render an empire obsolete. Competing nations or external forces that embrace technological progress may outpace the empire, leading to a decline in influence.

6. Environmental Degradation: Empires often exploit natural resources for economic gain. However, unchecked exploitation and environmental degradation can have long-term consequences. Deforestation, soil erosion, and pollution can impact agriculture, exacerbating economic challenges and contributing to societal decline.

7. External Pressures and Military Defeats: Encounters with external forces, whether through invasions, conflicts, or geopolitical shifts, can challenge the dominance of empires. Military defeats or geopolitical

realignments may weaken an empire's standing on the global stage, leading to a loss of territories or influence.

8. Cultural and Ideological Erosion: The erosion of cultural and ideological cohesion can contribute to the decline of empires. When the founding principles and values that once bound diverse cultures together begin to unravel, a sense of identity and purpose may wane, impacting the empire's ability to inspire loyalty and unity.

The decline of empires is often a complex interplay of these factors, and their manifestation can vary across different historical contexts.

Chapter 14

Echoes of Empires

A Reflection on America Today

As we navigate the annals of history, the rise and fall of empires unfold before us like a timeless epic. The Chinese, Spanish, French, English, and American empires, each with its unique saga, offer profound insights into the ebb and flow of power, influence, and societal dynamics.

Yet, as we immerse ourselves in this grand narrative, it is not merely a historical tapestry we behold but a mirror reflecting the complexities of the present. America, the torchbearer of modern civilization, stands at a crossroads, and the echoes of empires past reverberate through its corridors of power.

The very fabric of empires is woven with threads of economic ascendancy and decline. The lessons from the rise and fall of these mighty realms beckon us to ponder the economic landscape of America today. How does the nation navigate global trade, fiscal responsibility, and the evolving contours of wealth and prosperity? As we delve into the echoes of economic stewardship, we find ourselves questioning the foundations upon which empires are built.

Military prowess, a defining attribute of empires, dances on the precipice of both triumph and hubris. The tales of military overreach in history's archives caution us to tread with wisdom. In an era of global interconnectedness, how does America wield its military might? Does it avoid the pitfalls of overextension and prioritize diplomatic solutions? The echoes of martial expeditions compel us to reflect on the role of America in today's geopolitical theater.

Internally, empires grapple with the forces of unity and dissent. The lessons of internal discord prompt us to examine America's societal tapestry. How does the nation reconcile diversity and address internal disparities? Does it foster a sense of unity that transcends differences, or does it risk succumbing to the fractures that have undermined empires before? As we explore the echoes of internal unity, we find ourselves contemplating the resilience of America's social fabric.

Administrative integrity, technological vigilance, environmental stewardship, global engagement, and cultural cohesion—each facet of empires' ascent and decline holds a mirror to America's current state. The reader is invited to wander through the corridors of history, pondering the shared patterns that bind the fate of empires with the destiny of the United States.

In the tapestry of time, the threads of empires intertwine with the present moment. The rise and fall of these grand civilizations pose questions that echo through the ages. As America stands at the crossroads of history, the reader is left to wonder about the choices that shape its destiny. What lessons will be drawn from the echoes of empires, and how will the story of America unfold in the chapters yet to be written?

Chapter 15

The Power of Insight

America's Unique Privilege

In the vast tapestry of history, the American empire holds a unique privilege—one that distinguishes it from the empires of antiquity. This privilege lies in the unparalleled access to a wealth of data, historical content, and the ability to glean insights from the rise and fall of civilizations. As we navigate the corridors of time, the question arises: How can America leverage this treasure trove of knowledge to not only understand its trajectory but to alter the course of its own narrative?

1. A Tapestry of Knowledge: The digital age has bestowed upon America an unprecedented tapestry of knowledge. The vast repositories of historical records, the collective wisdom of human experience, and the intricacies of past empires are at its fingertips. This wealth of information serves as a compass, offering insights into the dynamics that have shaped the rise and fall of civilizations.

2. Reading the Past to Guess the Future: The ability to read the past is a formidable tool in deciphering the future. By delving into the annals of history, America can identify patterns, understand the consequences of past decisions, and anticipate the challenges that lie ahead. The phrase "By

reading the past to guess the future" becomes a guiding principle, allowing for informed decision-making and strategic planning.

3. Navigating the Crossroads: America, standing at the crossroads of its own narrative, possesses the means to navigate with clarity. The lessons drawn from the decline of empires offer a compass for avoiding pitfalls. By recognizing the factors that led to decline in the past, America can chart a course that steers clear of those pitfalls, fostering resilience and adaptability.

4. Adaptive Governance: One of the privileges afforded by historical insights is the ability to adapt governance structures. By learning from the administrative successes and failures of past empires, America can fortify its institutions. Transparent, accountable, and efficient governance becomes the cornerstone for steering the ship of state through the complexities of the modern era.

5. Technological Innovation: The digital age has not only provided access to historical knowledge but has also accelerated technological innovation. America's unique privilege lies in its ability to harness these innovations for societal progress. From artificial intelligence to sustainable technologies, the tools to propel the nation forward are within reach.

6. Environmental Stewardship: Environmental challenges that befell past empires can be met with a proactive stance. Armed with data and insights, America can champion environmental stewardship. Sustainable

practices, conservation efforts, and global initiatives can mitigate the ecological strains that have contributed to the decline of civilizations.

7. Global Collaboration: The interconnectedness of the world today allows America to engage in global collaboration with a depth unseen in history. By learning from the diplomatic successes and failures of past empires, the nation can forge alliances, navigate geopolitical shifts, and contribute to a world order that fosters peace and stability.

8. Fostering Cultural Cohesion: America's diverse cultural landscape is a source of strength. Drawing from historical lessons, the nation can foster cultural cohesion while embracing diversity. Inclusivity, mutual respect, and a shared commitment to core values become the glue that binds a nation in times of challenge.

As America stands on the precipice of the future, the privilege of access to vast data and historical content becomes a powerful ally. The narrative that unfolds depends on the wisdom with which this privilege is wielded—a testament to the idea that by understanding the past, a nation can shape its destiny.

Chapter 16

The Evolution of Power

Smart Diplomacy and Global Harmony

As the United States of America stands at the crossroads of a rapidly evolving world, the path forward requires a nuanced and intelligent approach. In the digital age, where information flows seamlessly across borders, the traditional paradigms of power are undergoing a transformation. To shape a future of peace, stability, and unprecedented diplomacy, America must embark on a journey that redefines its interactions with the world.

1. Technological Diplomacy: The evolution of power in the 21st century demands a technological renaissance in diplomacy. Harnessing the power of artificial intelligence, big data analytics, and advanced communication technologies can elevate diplomatic efforts. Technological diplomacy becomes the cornerstone for fostering understanding, cooperation, and conflict resolution.

2. Inclusive Policy Development: The traditional top-down approach to policy development needs a metamorphosis. Inclusivity should be at the heart of crafting policies that resonate with the diverse perspectives of a globalized world. By incorporating voices from various cultures and

ideologies, America can create policies that are not only effective but also respectful of the diversity within and beyond its borders.

3. Cultural Respect and Understanding: Respecting the cultures and different ways of thinking of other nations is a fundamental tenet of smart diplomacy. America's diplomatic approach should be grounded in a genuine understanding and appreciation of the rich tapestry of global cultures. This cultural respect becomes a bridge for fostering connections, dispelling misconceptions, and building relationships based on mutual understanding.

4. Strategic Alliances: The era of zero-sum diplomacy is giving way to collaborative endeavors. Strategic alliances with competitors like Russia, China, Venezuela, Iran, and others should be forged through dialogue and shared interests. America can pioneer a new approach, emphasizing cooperation over confrontation, and seeking common ground even in areas of disagreement.

5. Economic Cooperation: Economic ties are potent instruments of diplomacy. By fostering economic cooperation, trade agreements, and partnerships, America can transcend political differences and build bridges of mutual prosperity. Economic interdependence becomes a stabilizing force, reducing the likelihood of conflicts and promoting shared interests.

6. Return to Diplomatic Wisdom: In the realm of international relations, the return to diplomatic wisdom is imperative. Drawing inspiration from figures like Henry Kissinger, America can champion a diplomacy rooted in

strategic insight, long-term vision, and the art of negotiation. Guns should only be a last resort, with dialogue and negotiation serving as the primary tools of conflict resolution.

7. Diplomacy in the Digital Age: The digital age offers unprecedented opportunities for diplomatic engagement. Social media, online forums, and digital platforms can be harnessed to facilitate cross-cultural dialogues, citizen diplomacy, and real-time communication. Leveraging technology in this way enables a more direct and inclusive form of diplomacy.

8. A Paradigm Shift in Global Leadership: America's pursuit of world peace and stability requires a paradigm shift in global leadership. Instead of imposing ideologies, a humble and collaborative leadership style can inspire trust and cooperation. By respecting the sovereignty of other nations and embracing a posture of humility, America can lead by example.

As America redefines its role on the world stage, the guiding principles of smart diplomacy, technological innovation, cultural respect, and a commitment to peace can pave the way for a future where nations collaborate, understand, and thrive together. In this era of interconnectedness, the power of diplomacy becomes not just a tool for national interest but a force for global harmony.

Chapter 17

The Power of Now

A Call for Individual Awakening

In the grand tapestry of global change, the most potent catalyst often emerges at the smallest, most intimate level—the individual. The heartbeat of nations is synchronized with the collective pulse of its people. To embark on a journey of unprecedented diplomacy and cultural understanding, the call must echo from the individual to the nation and beyond.

1. The Individual as the Epicenter: Change commences with the individual—an awareness that each person holds within them the power to shape the future. The recognition that life unfolds in a series of ebbs and flows, and with this understanding, individuals become architects of their destiny.

2. Empowering Families: As the ripple of awareness spreads, it encompasses the family unit. Empowering families to instill resilience, adaptability, and a global perspective in the younger generation becomes a cornerstone. The family, as a microcosm of society, becomes a nurturing ground for enlightened individuals.

3. Building Resilient Societies: From families, the wave of change radiates to societies. Resilient societies are built upon the collective strength

of individuals who embrace life's uncertainties. Educational systems, community initiatives, and societal values should be aligned to foster not just academic knowledge but emotional intelligence and cultural appreciation.

4. A Nation of Enlightened Citizens: An enlightened nation is a collective of individuals who understand the ebb and flow of life, acknowledging that challenges are an inherent part of the human experience. The nation, in turn, becomes a force for good, a beacon of wisdom and understanding on the global stage.

5. The Urgency of Now: The call for change is not a distant whisper; it's an urgent plea for action in the present. Now is the time for every American to grasp the reins of their destiny, to understand that delays and procrastination only postpone the inevitable. Providence is the best medicine, and the time for transformation is now.

6. No Room for Delay and Laziness: In the pursuit of a better future, there is no room for delays or laziness. Procrastination becomes the enemy of progress. Each moment, each decision, holds the potential to reshape destinies. The urgency of the present demands a proactive and purposeful approach.

7. Embracing Providence: Providence, often seen as the silent guide of destiny, takes center stage in times of change. Embracing providence is not a passive surrender but an active acknowledgment of the opportunities

presented in every challenge. It is an understanding that adversity can be a catalyst for growth and transformation.

8. The Power of Collective Action: The transformation from the individual to the nation is not a solitary journey but a collective endeavor. The power of now resides in the hands of every American, and as they unite in purpose, their collective actions become a formidable force for change.

Now, as the call resonates from the individual to the nation, the power of now becomes the fulcrum upon which the destiny of America pivots. The journey of unprecedented diplomacy, cultural respect, and global harmony starts with the realization that each individual is an agent of change—a custodian of the future.

Chapter 18
The Triumph of Clarity

Critical Thinking and Vision for the Future

In the ever-evolving landscape of the 21st century, the survival and flourishing of individuals and nations hinge upon the virtues of critical thinking, logical reasoning, and an unwavering commitment to honesty—both with oneself and as a collective. This chapter delves into the crucible of clarity, examining how these principles can be the guiding light for navigating the complexities of the future.

1. Critical Thinking as a Beacon: Critical thinking is not merely a skill; it is a beacon illuminating the path of sound decision-making. Individuals who cultivate this ability possess the power to dissect information, discern truth from misinformation, and make informed choices. Likewise, nations that foster critical thinking among their citizens build a resilient foundation for the challenges that lie ahead.

2. Logical Reasoning in a Turbulent World: In a world characterized by rapid changes and interconnected challenges, logical reasoning becomes a linchpin for navigating uncertainty. The ability to analyze situations objectively, connect disparate dots, and devise strategic solutions is the hallmark of a society ready to face the intricacies of the future.

3. Honesty with Oneself: The foundation of personal and collective growth rests on the bedrock of honesty with oneself. Individuals who introspect, acknowledge strengths and weaknesses, and embrace personal truths lay the groundwork for continuous improvement. A nation that encourages self-reflection cultivates citizens with the moral fortitude to confront challenges with honesty.

4. The Ripple Effect of Individual Honesty: The honesty of individuals creates a ripple effect that resonates through society. As citizens engage in open dialogue and transparent communication, a culture of trust emerges. In this environment, the seeds of collective progress are sown, and the nation becomes a beacon of integrity on the global stage.

5. Clarity of Vision: The survival and flourishing of individuals and nations are intrinsically tied to having a clear vision. Individuals with a sense of purpose, guided by personal values and a vision for their future, are better equipped to weather storms and capitalize on opportunities. Nations that articulate and collectively embrace a clear vision steer a course towards prosperity.

6. Adaptability as a Virtue: A clear vision does not imply rigidity; rather, it demands adaptability. Individuals and nations alike must possess the agility to adjust their course in response to changing circumstances. The ability to adapt, coupled with a clear vision, creates a dynamic synergy that propels growth in the face of uncertainty.

7. Collective Wisdom for Global Challenges: The global challenges of the future require collective wisdom. Nations that pool their intellectual resources, foster collaboration, and engage in diplomatic discourse based on critical thinking and logical reasoning are better positioned to address complex issues. The triumph of clarity emerges when nations unite to solve shared challenges.

8. Education as the Catalyst: The cultivation of critical thinking, logical reasoning, honesty, and a clear vision begins in the crucible of education. A robust educational system becomes the catalyst for nurturing these virtues in individuals, empowering them to contribute meaningfully to the progress of their nation and the world.

In the crucible of clarity, where critical thinking, logical reasoning, honesty, and a clear vision converge, individuals and nations forge the tools not just to survive but to flourish in the unpredictable terrain of the future. This chapter invites a reflection on these virtues as the keys to unlocking a future defined by resilience, progress, and collective well-being.

Chapter 19
Blooming Unity

Overcoming Divisions for Personal and Collective Prosperity

As we navigate the intricacies of the modern world, it becomes increasingly apparent that divisions—be they based on race, religion, tribal affiliations, or any other artificial constructs—are impediments to the flourishing of individuals and the health of the collective environment. This chapter delves into the transformative power of unity, exploring how the harmony within oneself, the family, and the nation can foster an ecosystem where prosperity blooms.

1. The Detrimental Impact of Divisions: Divisions, whether rooted in superficial differences or deep-seated prejudices, create fractures within the human experience. They breed discord, stifle progress, and hinder the collective pursuit of prosperity. Recognizing the detrimental impact of divisions is the first step toward cultivating a more harmonious existence.

2. Unity within the Self: True unity begins within the individual. Harmony within oneself—the integration of mind, body, and spirit—forms the bedrock of personal well-being. As individuals embark on a journey of self-discovery, they shed the divisive layers that hinder personal growth, paving the way for a more authentic and fulfilling life.

3. The Family as a Nexus of Unity: The family unit, when united by bonds of love, respect, and understanding, becomes a nexus of unity. It serves as a crucible where individuals learn the value of cooperation, empathy, and shared goals. A harmonious family fosters a nurturing environment for personal development and collective prosperity.

4. Overcoming National Divisions: Extending unity beyond the family, the nation emerges as a collective entity where diverse individuals unite under a common identity. Overcoming divisions at the national level involves fostering inclusivity, embracing diversity, and acknowledging the shared humanity that transcends superficial differences.

5. The Ecosystem of Collective Prosperity: In a society where unity prevails, a flourishing ecosystem of collective prosperity takes root. Individuals from diverse backgrounds contribute their unique perspectives and skills, creating a synergy that propels the nation forward. The health of this ecosystem is directly linked to the strength of the unity that binds its constituents.

6. Nurturing the Seeds of Understanding: Nurturing unity requires cultivating the seeds of understanding. Encouraging open dialogue, promoting cultural exchange, and fostering empathy are essential steps in overcoming divisions. As individuals and nations understand and appreciate one another, the barriers that once stood as divisive forces begin to crumble.

7. Transcending Superficial Divisions: Superficial divisions, whether based on appearance, beliefs, or affiliations, crumble in the face of genuine unity. As individuals and nations transcend these surface-level differences, they uncover the shared aspirations and common humanity that bind them together. Unity becomes a powerful force that transcends the limitations of divisive constructs.

8. The Blooming of Prosperity: As unity takes root within individuals, families, and nations, a remarkable transformation occurs—a blooming of prosperity on both personal and collective levels. This prosperity extends beyond material wealth, encompassing emotional well-being, social harmony, and a shared sense of purpose.

In the journey toward personal and collective prosperity, the eradication of divisions is not just a lofty ideal; it is an essential prerequisite. This chapter invites readers to reflect on the transformative power of unity and the potential for blooming prosperity when individuals, families, and nations unite in the pursuit of a harmonious existence.

Chapter 20

Unveiling Realities

Navigating the Landscape of Corporatocracy

In the spirit of critical thinking and an open dialogue, let us embark on a journey together—an exploration that challenges preconceptions and ventures into the realm of political realities. We often hold dear the notion that the United States operates as a bastion of democracy, a system where the people's voices shape the course of the nation. However, as we peel back the layers of political intricacies, a different reality unveils itself—one that calls for honest reflection and a departure from idealistic illusions.

1. The Myth of Democracy: In theory, democracy is a beacon of collective governance, a system where the voice of the people resonates through the corridors of power. However, the stark truth is that practical democracy, as envisioned by its philosophical architects, remains elusive. The reality we face is a departure from the democratic ideals professed in theory.

2. The Emergence of Corporatocracy: What we confront in the United States is the rise of corporatocracy—a system where the influence of powerful corporations extends far beyond the marketplace into the very fabric of governance. The symbiotic relationship between political

establishments and corporate interests shapes policies, decisions, and the trajectory of the nation.

3. Funding the Future Leaders: A critical examination of political landscapes reveals a web of financial entanglements where corporations strategically subsidize future presidents, administrations, and political campaigns. The strings attached to such financial support weave a narrative of indebtedness, where elected officials may prioritize the interests of their funders over the collective will of the people.

4. The Illusion of Choice: As voters, we participate in an electoral process that presents the illusion of choice. Behind the curtain, however, a select group of corporations, often with overlapping interests, subsidizes both major political parties. The result is a mirage of opposition, where the lines between Democrats and Republicans blur in service to shared corporate backers.

5. Debunking Partisan Allegiances: Partisan allegiances, once believed to represent fundamental ideological differences, reveal themselves as more nuanced. The same corporations that fund one party extend their influence across the aisle. The subtle orchestration of political theater belies the notion of a genuine clash of ideas and principles.

6. A Call for Critical Thinking: In the face of these revelations, a call for critical thinking emerges. As readers, as citizens, we must navigate the political landscape with discernment. We must question narratives,

scrutinize funding sources, and reevaluate the notion that our electoral choices manifest in true representation.

7. An Open Mind for Unveiling Truths: To embark on this exploration requires an open mind—an openness to unveil uncomfortable truths that may challenge our established beliefs. The commitment to critical thinking is not an act of rebellion but a quest for a more authentic understanding of the forces shaping our nation.

8. A Path to Informed Citizenship: As we traverse this landscape together, the goal is not disillusionment but empowerment—an empowerment that stems from an informed citizenship. By understanding the dynamics of corporatocracy, we pave the way for collective action, demanding a reevaluation of systems that may have strayed from the democratic ideals we hold dear.

In the spirit of openness and critical reflection, let us venture into the heart of our political reality. The journey toward informed citizenship requires not just questioning the status quo but actively participating in reshaping it for the collective well-being of the nation.

Chapter 21

The Enigma of Opportunity

Unveiling the Benevolent Dictatorship

The term "dictator" carries with it a heavy historical burden, often invoking images of oppressive regimes and unchecked power. However, a closer examination of its roots reveals a more nuanced understanding, challenging the common perception that all dictators are tyrants.

The word "dictator" finds its origins in ancient Rome, derived from the Latin "dictator," meaning 'one who dictates.' In the Roman context, a dictator was appointed during times of crisis, bestowed with absolute authority to make decisive decisions for the greater good of the state. This form of leadership aimed at preserving the republic during emergencies and was not intended for perpetual rule.

Delving deeper into ancient Greek, the term "dictator" is absent, but the concept of a singular leader emerges. The Greek word "autokrator" (αὐτοκράτωρ) signifies a ruler with self-derived power, emphasizing the capacity for independent decision-making.

Two leaders from different times and cultures exemplify how dictatorial powers, when wielded with concern, love, and devotion, can contribute significantly to the common good.

In antiquity, Marcus Aurelius, a Roman Emperor and Stoic philosopher, rose to power reluctantly during a period of crisis. His leadership was marked by a commitment to the well-being of his people, emphasizing justice, wisdom, and benevolence. Aurelius steered the Roman Empire through challenges with a focus on the greater good, leaving a legacy that transcends his time.

In modern times, Lee Kuan Yew, the founding father of Singapore, assumed dictatorial powers in the early years of the nation's independence. However, his leadership was characterized by a vision for economic development, social stability, and the common good. Under his rule, Singapore transformed from a struggling state into a global economic powerhouse, demonstrating the potential positive impact of dictatorial powers when wielded responsibly.

While the term "dictator" may evoke negative connotations, the historical context and the examples of leaders like Marcus Aurelius and Lee Kuan Yew underscore that dictatorship is not inherently malicious. Leadership, when guided by a genuine concern for the common good, can yield positive outcomes even in seemingly autocratic systems. Understanding the complexities of dictatorial power invites us to reevaluate our preconceptions and recognize that, in certain instances, dictatorship can be a force for good.

However, it's crucial to acknowledge that dictators, like any leaders, are fallible. Mistakes can be made, as seen in contemporary history with leaders like Augusto Pinochet of Chile and Fidel Castro of Cuba. Despite their potentially good intentions, their policies led to grave errors, emphasizing the need for caution and accountability in wielding dictatorial powers. This acknowledgment underscores the importance of learning from history to ensure that the mistakes of the past are not repeated in the pursuit of the common good.

In the intricate dance of power and opportunity, the United States of America emerges as an enigma—an embodiment of both the survival of the fittest and the ascent of the smartest. Beneath the façade of democracy, a subtle current flows, steering the nation toward a unique amalgamation of prosperity and dominance. Let us unravel the layers of this enigma and explore how, perhaps, the land of opportunity has birthed a breed of benevolent dictators.

1. The Land of Opportunity: The narrative of the United States as the land of opportunity is etched into the cultural fabric of the nation. A place where dreams are pursued and fortunes are made, the U.S. symbolizes the promise that anyone, regardless of background, can ascend to greatness. Yet, woven into this tapestry is an undercurrent that elevates not only the fittest but the smartest.

2. Survival of the Smartest: Nature's law of survival of the fittest finds a peculiar echo in the American experience. Here, the definition of fitness expands beyond physical prowess to include intellectual acuity and strategic thinking. The nation seems to embrace the idea that the smartest, those adept at navigating the complex currents of power, dominate and shape the destiny of the land.

3. The Benevolence of Dictatorship: Behind the veiled curtain of democracy, a form of benevolent dictatorship takes shape—a subtle orchestration where the heavyweights, the intellectual titans, don the mask of democracy. The brilliance lies in the art of governance that, while draped in democratic principles, allows for a certain form of enlightened rule.

4. The Masks We Wear: The masks we wear, whether as individuals or as a nation, often reveal more than they conceal. The mask of democracy, worn by the heavyweights of intellect, serves as a vessel for societal harmony and progress. It is not a dictatorship rooted in tyranny but a strategic governance that steers the ship with a keen awareness of the nation's needs.

5. Opportunities and Predators: Opportunity, in the context of the U.S., is a double-edged sword. It propels individuals to greatness, but it also begets a landscape where the intellectually adept can ascend to positions of influence. The nation, in embracing this dynamic, weaves a narrative where

the smartest become benevolent predators, shepherding the collective destiny.

6. A Symbiosis of Power and Progress: The symbiosis of power and progress is the heartbeat of this benevolent dictatorship. The heavyweights, while asserting their influence, also become stewards of societal advancement. It is a delicate balance where the pursuit of personal and collective well-being intertwines, creating a narrative that defies conventional notions of governance.

7. A Unique Magic: In this enigma lies a unique magic—the ability of the heavyweights to wear the cloak of democracy while steering the ship with an astute hand. The nation, under the guidance of these benevolent dictators, charts a course that, in its essence, blends the Darwinian principle of survival with the intellectual prowess that defines the smartest.

8. The Evolutionary Tapestry: As we reflect on this narrative, we witness the evolution of a nation that, knowingly or unknowingly, follows the threads of nature's tapestry. The U.S., the land of opportunity, embraces not only the fittest but thc smartest, giving rise to a form of governance that, for better or worse, shapes the destiny of a nation and its people.

In this exploration, we peel back the layers of the American experience, acknowledging the complexity that defines the nation's trajectory. The emergence of benevolent dictators, donned in the guise of democracy, adds a nuanced dimension to the narrative of the land of opportunity.

Chapter 22

Navigating the Abyss

The Imperative for Corporate Socialism

In the uncharted territories of economic evolution, a paradox unfolds—a potential shift toward corporate socialism driven not by altruism but by the stark reality of survival. As the chasm between the affluent and the disenfranchised widens, the custodians of capital find themselves standing at a crossroads where adaptation becomes a matter of necessity. In this chapter, we explore the improbable but conceivable scenario where even giants like Google, Microsoft, Amazon, Apple and metaverse must recalibrate their strategies, not out of benevolence, but as a pragmatic means of securing their own survival.

1. The Widening Gulf of Inequality: In the relentless pursuit of profit, the gap between the economic elites and the broader populace has expanded into an abyss. As societal resentment simmers, a realization dawns upon the owners of capital—a reality where the survival of their enterprises is inexorably linked to the well-being and contentment of the masses.

2. The Uncharted Realm of Corporate Socialism: To navigate the abyss of growing inequality, the captains of industry find themselves contemplating an unthinkable proposition—embracing elements of socialism within the capitalist framework. Not driven by an epiphany of

empathy, but by a stark understanding that a system teetering on the brink of social unrest jeopardizes not only profits but the very survival of corporate empires.

3. Survival as the Catalyst: The impetus for corporate socialism is not an ideological awakening but an elemental survival instinct. The recognition that unchecked inequality breeds discontent, instability, and the potential for upheaval forces even the staunchest proponents of capitalism to reevaluate their strategies.

4. Redistribution as a Strategic Imperative: The redistribution of wealth, once anathema to capitalist principles, emerges as a strategic imperative. Corporations, now navigating the delicate terrain of societal harmony, divert a fraction of their immense fortunes to social causes, educational systems, and charitable endeavors. It is not philanthropy born of generosity but a calculated maneuver to assuage societal grievances.

5. Mitigating the Grudge: In the face of a populace burdened by economic disparities, corporations recognize the need to mitigate the grudge that festers within thc hearts of citizens. By actively participating in social welfare initiatives, they seek to transform their image from detached behemoths to entities invested in the well-being of the very communities that sustain them.

6. The Strange Dance of Survival: The dance between capitalism and socialism, once seen as opposing forces, takes on a strange harmony in this

new paradigm. Survival demands a delicate balance—a capitalist system that acknowledges the necessity of socialist measures to ensure its own perpetuity.

7. The Metaverse and Social Responsibility: Even in the burgeoning realms of the metaverse, where digital empires amass unprecedented wealth, the specter of societal responsibility looms. The pioneers of these virtual domains, too, may find themselves compelled to contribute to the social fabric, not as an act of altruism but as a pragmatic step toward securing the longevity of their metaversal domains.

8. The Pragmatism of Corporate Survival: As corporations embark on this unprecedented journey into corporate socialism, it is crucial to understand that their motives are not born of a newfound moral compass but of the pragmatism required for survival. The outcome, however, could be a transformative force that reshapes the narrative of capitalism, not through revolution, but through the evolutionary dance of adaptation.

In this chapter, we delve into the paradoxical prospect where even the titans of capitalism are compelled to adopt socialist measures for reasons not rooted in ideology but in the stark necessity of survival.

Chapter 23

Embracing the Acceleration

Navigating the Era of Artificial Intelligence

In the relentless cadence of time, our world hurtles forward at an unprecedented pace. What once held true, the certainties we clung to, are now but echoes in the ever-changing symphony of existence. It is imperative, now more than ever, for Americans to embark on a profound reevaluation of values, a recalibration of perspectives, and an opening of minds to the demands of the present and the uncertainties of the future.

1. The Acceleration of Our World: With each passing day, the velocity of our world accelerates. The familiar landscapes of yesterday transform into uncharted territories, demanding a constant reassessment of our values and a nimble adaptation to the evolving currents of reality.

2. A Call for Critical Thinking: To navigate the complexities of our accelerating world, the call for critical thinking reverberates. It is a clarion call to question, to analyze, and to respond not based on outdated notions but in alignment with the exigencies of the now.

3. Artificial Intelligence: A Transformative Force: At the heart of this accelerated reality lies the imminent arrival of artificial intelligence—a force that will not only shake the foundations of humanity but redefine the

very fabric of our civilization. The challenge is not to fear this inevitability but to embrace it, recognizing AI as one of the most powerful tools ever invented by humankind.

4. Readiness for Big Changes: To secure our civilization's survival and flourishing, we must be ready for monumental shifts. The familiar must be relinquished, and the unexplored embraced. The future demands a courage to confront the unknown, to adapt, and to propel ourselves forward.

5. Openness to the Challenges of the Times: Openness to the challenges of the times becomes a mantra for progress. It is an acknowledgment that the status quo is but a fleeting moment, and the challenges of today are the stepping stones toward a future we can shape if we possess the will to confront them.

6. Bridging the Past, Present, and Future: The richness of our generation, unparalleled in history, is a legacy that carries the weight of responsibility. It necessitates a delicate dance—a bridge between the lessons of the past, the intensity of the present, and the unfolding vistas of the future.

7. Artificial Intelligence as a Catalyst: Artificial intelligence, a potent catalyst for change, should be viewed not as a threat but as an ally. It is a tool that, when wielded with wisdom, has the potential to elevate humanity to new heights. Our gratitude for being the richest generation overall should

translate into a determination to harness AI for the well-being of ourselves and future generations.

8. Marching into the Future: With an open mind, fortified by critical thinking, we march into the future. It is a journey marked by the acknowledgment that the landscapes we traverse are in constant flux. Our resilience and adaptability become the compass, guiding us through the uncharted realms of possibility.

In this chapter, we stand at the crossroads of acceleration and transformation. The key is not just to survive but to flourish—to seize the opportunities embedded in the challenges, to welcome the power of artificial intelligence, and to propel our civilization into a future that we, with open minds and determined spirits, can shape.

Chapter 24

Breaking the Chains

Toward a Future of Boundless Horizons

As we stand at the threshold of a new era, it's time to cast aside the antiquated narratives that have confined us—stories of religious divides, political partisanship, and racial tensions. Let us collectively move forward, fueled by optimism and driven by audacious goals that promise not just survival, but a flourishing existence. This chapter is a rallying call for humanity to break free from the chains of old paradigms and stride boldly toward a future adorned with limitless horizons.

1. Liberation from Antiquated Narratives: The shackles of antiquated narratives—be they rooted in religious, political, or racial divisions—have restrained humanity for far too long. It's time to liberate ourselves from these confinements and step into the uncharted territories of a world unburdened by the weight of divisive stories.

2. Forward with Optimism: Optimism becomes our guiding light, illuminating the path toward a future brimming with possibilities. It is not a naïve hope but a pragmatic belief that, with determination and collective effort, we can overcome challenges and carve a destiny that surpasses the limitations of the past.

3. Big Goals for Human Flourishing: Our goals must transcend the mundane and embrace the monumental. It's not merely about survival but about human flourishing—a state where every individual thrives, where life becomes a canvas painted with the vibrant hues of accomplishment, fulfillment, and shared prosperity.

4. Easing the Stocks of Survival Issues: While pursuing grand aspirations, we must not neglect the basics. The stocks of survival—access to clean water, ample food, healthcare, and shelter—must be made abundant and accessible to all. It is a foundational step toward building a future where every person can dream beyond mere survival.

5. Richer with Open Horizons: The richness we seek goes beyond material abundance; it encompasses the wealth of open horizons. It is about expanding our collective consciousness, fostering curiosity, and unlocking the vast potential within every individual. A richness that stems from knowledge, understanding, and the shared exploration of the wonders that lie ahead.

6. Evolution as the Guiding Principle: Evolution becomes our guiding principle. It is not just a biological concept but a philosophy that propels us forward. The evolution of thought, of systems, of compassion—each layer contributing to the grand tapestry of human progress.

7. Leaving a Legacy of Ease: In our pursuit, let us strive to leave a legacy of ease for future generations. Ease in solving problems, ease in accessing

knowledge, ease in coexisting harmoniously. It is the gift we bestow upon the continuum of humanity—a world where the journey is not burdened by unnecessary complexities.

8. Flourishing in the Tapestry of Time: As we break free from the chains of old narratives, as we stride boldly toward audacious goals, we become weavers in the tapestry of time. Our actions ripple through generations, creating a narrative that speaks not of divisions and strife but of a humanity that flourished, evolved, and embraced the boundless horizons of possibility.

This chapter marks a departure from the constraints of the past, a leap into a future where optimism, audacious goals, and a commitment to human flourishing propel us toward horizons yet unexplored.

Chapter 25
The Strength in Humility

A New Paradigm of Superiority

In the annals of history, empires and civilizations often clung to the illusion of superiority, a megalomania that echoed through time. Yet, in the tapestry of our shared humanity, let us chart a new course—one marked not by claims of superiority but by the strength found in humility. This chapter explores the transformative power of admitting our imperfections, embracing humility as a nation and as a people. Let our openness become a beacon, an example that sets us apart, not in false superiority, but in the genuine pursuit of a better tomorrow for all humanity.

1. The Illusion of Superiority: Through the ages, empires and civilizations draped themselves in the illusion of superiority. The echoes of grandeur reverberated in claims of exceptionalism, yet history teaches us that such assertions often led to hubris and downfall.

2. A Paradigm Shift: Let us embark on a paradigm shift—one that rejects the conventional notion of superiority. Instead, we find strength in acknowledging our imperfections, embracing humility as a guiding principle in our interactions with the world.

3. The Courage to Admit Imperfection: Admitting imperfection requires courage—a recognition that we, as a nation and as a people, are not immune to flaws. In this vulnerability lies a unique strength that sets the stage for genuine growth and connection.

4. Leading by Example: Our willingness to admit our imperfections becomes a beacon—a leadership by example. It is a departure from the historical pattern of grandiosity, offering a refreshing narrative that resonates with authenticity and resonates with other cultures.

5. The Cretan Thinking: Embracing humility is akin to the Cretan thinking—the paradoxical acknowledgment that wisdom lies in recognizing our limitations. This thinking becomes a cornerstone, an innovative approach that sets us apart not in claims of superiority but in the humility to learn from others.

6. The Open Mind: An open mind becomes our compass. It is the conduit through which ideas flow, cultures intertwine, and innovation flourishes. Our openness becomes a testament to a new form of superiority—a superiority rooted in the genuine pursuit of knowledge and progress.

7. Real Concern for a Better Tomorrow: Our humility is not a mere posture but a genuine concern for a better tomorrow—for all of humanity. It transcends borders and cultural divides, fostering collaborations that seek to address global challenges collectively.

8. The Sign of True Superiority: In this humility, in this willingness to admit imperfection, we discover a sign of true superiority. It is not a superiority that claims dominance but one that radiates from the depth of genuine concern, an openness to learn, and the audacity to forge a path toward a shared, harmonious future.

This chapter invites us to redefine our notion of superiority, to discard the illusions of grandeur, and to find strength in the humility that can shape a new narrative—one that transcends borders and fosters a genuine concern for the collective well-being of humanity.

Chapter 26

The Power of Benevolent Conquest

Redefining Greatness

As we stand at the pinnacle of power, a unique opportunity unfolds—a chance to become benevolent conquerors, not in the traditional sense of taking, but in the extraordinary act of giving. This chapter delves into the transformative potential of redefining our greatness as a nation, acknowledging that true superiority lies not in the art of taking, but in the audacity to give. It is a call to reevaluate our values, to summon the courage and strength required to embark on a legacy that transcends generations—a legacy of benevolence that echoes through the annals of history.

1. The Unprecedented Power to Give: In our hands lies an unprecedented power—the power to become conquerors who give instead of taking. This paradigm shift challenges the conventional notions of greatness and conquest, setting the stage for a legacy that reverberates through time.

2. Gratitude as the Catalyst: Much like the sun that gifts us with its radiant energy every day, our benevolence stems from a deep sense of gratitude. Gratitude becomes the catalyst for a new era of conquest—one where giving is not an obligation, but a manifestation of our abundance and appreciation.

3. Courage to Reevaluate: Before we embark on this transformative journey, we must summon the courage to reevaluate some fundamental aspects within ourselves. It requires introspection, a willingness to challenge ingrained beliefs, and the openness to embrace a new narrative of conquest—one defined by generosity.

4. Strength to Give: True strength lies not in amassing power for its own sake, but in harnessing that power to uplift others. The strength to give is a formidable force that propels us beyond the realms of traditional conquest, forging a path toward a greatness rooted in compassion and selflessness.

5. Benevolence as a Sign of Superiority: In the act of benevolent conquest, we carve out a legacy that stands as a sign of true superiority. It is a superiority not marked by the subjugation of others but by the elevation of the collective human spirit—a distinction that sets us apart in the pages of history.

6. Transformative Leadership: Our journey as benevolent conquerors demands transformative leadership—an unwavering commitment to lead with empathy, to inspire with compassion, and to navigate the complexities of global influence with a moral compass that points toward the betterment of humanity.

7. A Legacy Beyond Taking: The legacy we aspire to leave is one that transcends the age-old tales of conquest and dominance. It is a legacy beyond taking, beyond the echoes of empires built on the spoils of others.

It is a legacy built on the enduring principle that true greatness emerges when power is wielded not for personal gain, but for the enrichment of all.

8. Going Down in History as Something Special: As we chart this uncharted territory of benevolent conquest, we do so with the awareness that we are creating something special—something that will go down in history not as conquerors who plundered, but as benevolent leaders who gave generously to secure a better future for all humanity.

This chapter beckons us to redefine our understanding of conquest and greatness, urging us to become benevolent conquerors whose power is harnessed for the greater good—a legacy that will endure through the ages.

Chapter 27

Building a Sustainable Future

The Blueprint for Social and Environmental Enterprises

In the pursuit of global well-being and environmental restoration, the role of business cannot be overstated. This chapter delves into the possibilities of harnessing America's vast capital resources to establish real social and environmental enterprises that benefit citizens globally while addressing pressing environmental concerns.

Unleashing America's Capital Power:

The United States possesses immense capital, and redirecting it towards sustainable ventures can usher in a new era of positive impact. Unlike traditional profit-centric models, these enterprises prioritize social and environmental responsibility, reflecting a commitment to creating a better world.

Learning from Successful Models:

Examining the success stories of franchises like McDonald's, Starbucks, and Coca-Cola provides valuable insights. These companies not only conquered the market but also became global icons. We can draw upon their strategies and adapt them to the creation of enterprises with a focus on social impact and environmental stewardship.

Identifying Key Sectors for Impact:

To make a substantial difference, social and environmental enterprises must target key sectors. These include renewable energy, sustainable agriculture, eco-friendly technologies, waste management, and initiatives fostering social equality and education. Strategic investments in these areas can yield long-term benefits for both society and the planet.

Collaboration and Innovation:

Real change comes through collaboration and innovation. By fostering partnerships with governments, NGOs, and other businesses, these enterprises can pool resources and expertise. Innovative solutions driven by cutting-edge technologies can create a positive domino effect, inspiring others to follow suit.

Global Expansion and Cultural Sensitivity:

Just as global franchises adapted to diverse cultures, social and environmental enterprises must embrace cultural sensitivity. Understanding local nuances ensures that initiatives resonate with communities worldwide, fostering acceptance and sustainability.

Transparency and Accountability:

Building trust is paramount. Social and environmental enterprises must be transparent in their operations, showcasing their commitment to ethical practices. Accountability mechanisms, such as third-party audits and reporting standards, can further solidify their credibility.

Long-Term Vision and Adaptability:

Sustainable enterprises need a long-term vision that extends beyond profit margins. They must anticipate future challenges, adapt to evolving circumstances, and demonstrate resilience. Flexibility in approach ensures continued relevance and impact.

Conclusion:

In conclusion, the establishment of social and environmental enterprises is not only a moral imperative but a strategic investment in a better future. By leveraging America's abundant capital, drawing inspiration from successful franchises, and adopting a global perspective, these enterprises can lead the way in addressing the world's most pressing challenges. The blueprint outlined in this chapter serves as a guide for entrepreneurs and visionaries to contribute to a sustainable and prosperous world for all.

Chapter 28
The Power of Abundance

Leveraging Economic Strength for Benevolence

In the realm of reality, as an American, the acknowledgment of abundance is a foundational truth. With the unique ability to create money, we stand at the intersection of economic strength and benevolent potential. This chapter explores the transformative power of leveraging our economic prowess to build strong foundations—a prerequisite to becoming benevolent conquerors who give more than they take.

1. The American Advantage: At the heart of our journey toward benevolent conquest lies a distinct advantage—an abundance that extends beyond material wealth. As Americans, we possess the power to create money, a unique tool that can be harnessed to shape a world where basic needs are not a privilege but a universal entitlement.

2. Printing Money as a Narrative of Abundance: The ability to print money is not just a pragmatic capability; it is a narrative of abundance. Unlike finite resources, money has the potential to be abundant, flowing to address the pressing needs of humanity. Bankers, in their storytelling prowess, have convinced the world of the value embedded in this narrative.

3. Building Strong Foundations: Before we can embark on benevolence, we recognize the necessity to build strong foundations. This involves a strategic exploitation of our economic strength—using the narrative of abundance to lay the groundwork for a world where every individual can thrive.

4. Exploiting Money for Ultimate Purpose: To exploit money for our ultimate purpose, we must redefine what that purpose entails. It goes beyond individual gain; it encompasses the elevation of the collective human experience. Money becomes a means, not an end, as we channel its abundance toward initiatives that transcend borders and benefit all.

5. Shaping a World of Entitlement: Our economic strength empowers us to shape a world where basic needs are not contingent on geographic location or socioeconomic status. It is a vision of entitlement—a recognition that every human being deserves clean air, sustenance, accessible water, and dignified shelter.

6. The Responsibility of Abundance: Abundance bears the weight of responsibility. It is not a license for unchecked exploitation but a call to wield our economic strength judiciously. The responsibility of abundance entails ensuring that the benefits of prosperity are distributed equitably.

7. Currency as a Tool for Change: The currency we possess, not just as a medium of exchange, but as a tool for change, becomes the instrument of benevolent conquest. As we print money, let it be an act that resonates with

the narrative of abundance—a narrative that seeks to uplift rather than hoard.

8. Pioneering the Path of Benevolence: In leveraging our economic strength for benevolence, we pioneer a path that defies conventional notions of conquest. It is a path where giving becomes a strategic exploitation of abundance—a legacy that echoes through generations, marking an era when prosperity was not an end in itself but a means to a more compassionate world.

This chapter illuminates the intersection of economic strength and benevolent potential, emphasizing the need to exploit our unique advantage to build strong foundations for a world where abundance is shared and basic needs are universal entitlements.

Chapter 29

Embracing the Future

America's Leadership in the Fourth Industrial Revolution

As we stand on the precipice of a transformative era, the Fourth Industrial Revolution beckons with the promise of unparalleled advancements. At its core are two potent tools—Artificial Intelligence (AI) and hydrogen fuel. This chapter unravels the narrative of America's leadership in this revolution, a journey that hinges on harnessing the power of AI, embracing the potential of hydrogen, and fostering a culture of continuous learning and adaptation.

1. The Fourth Industrial Revolution Unveiled: The Fourth Industrial Revolution is not a distant vision; it is the unfolding reality reshaping the landscape of our existence. At its helm are two formidable tools—Artificial Intelligence and hydrogen fuel—poised to catalyze a seismic shift in the way we live, work, and power our world.

2. The Role of Artificial Intelligence: Artificial Intelligence, a beacon of innovation, emerges not as an adversary to displace jobs but as a catalyst for a redefined workforce. Mundane tasks will yield to automation, paving the way for a surge in new, intellectually demanding roles. National

intelligence, coupled with continuous learning, becomes the key to unlocking the vast potential AI offers.

3. Hydrogen - The Fuel of Transformation: Hydrogen, the unsung hero, takes center stage as the fuel that will propel the Fourth Industrial Revolution. It marks the transition from fossil fuels to a sustainable energy era. Renewable sources, interconnected in a chain of innovation, will yield electricity that powers fuel cells, ultimately splitting water into hydrogen and oxygen.

4. The Obsolescence of Fossil Fuels: In the dance of progress, fossil fuels gracefully bow out as hydrogen steps into the limelight. The renewable energy symphony, conducted by wind, solar, geothermal, wave power, and human energy, creates a harmony that not only sustains but propels us into a future untethered from the shackles of environmentally taxing energy sources.

5. America's Financial and Technical Prowess: America, with its financial might and technological prowess, stands poised at the helm of the Fourth Industrial Revolution. The ability to lead hinges on a willingness to change course and embrace risk. The canvas of innovation awaits the strokes of American ingenuity to paint a picture of progress that resonates across borders.

6. Embracing Change and Risk: The path to leadership in the Fourth Industrial Revolution demands a cultural shift—an embrace of change and

a fearless approach to risk. In this era of rapid transformation, hesitancy becomes a barrier, while bold decisions become stepping stones to shaping the narrative of progress.

7. A Call to Continuous Learning: As the revolution unfolds, a call to arms echoes through the corridors of education—continuous learning becomes the currency of relevance. Adapting to new frontiers, exploring uncharted territories, and acquiring skills that align with the evolving technological landscape become the pillars of sustained leadership.

8. Crafting a Legacy of Innovation: America, with its unwavering spirit and pioneering ethos, has the opportunity to craft a legacy of innovation. The Fourth Industrial Revolution is not just a moment in time; it is an epoch where the trajectory of progress can be steered toward a future where technology serves humanity, sustains the planet, and fosters a global community united by progress.

This chapter paints a portrait of America's potential leadership in the Fourth Industrial Revolution, a narrative woven with the threads of AI, hydrogen fuel, and a commitment to continual learning and adaptation.

Chapter 30

A Strategic Blueprint for AI Leadership

Safeguarding Progress for America and the World

As America stands at the forefront of artificial intelligence (AI) development, it carries the responsibility to chart a strategic path that not only propels the nation to new heights but also safeguards the global community. This chapter outlines a comprehensive strategy for AI development, focusing on responsible innovation, ethical guidelines, and global collaboration to ensure the best and safest utilization of this transformative tool.

1. Prioritizing Responsible Innovation: The cornerstone of America's AI strategy lies in prioritizing responsible innovation. It involves fostering an environment that encourages breakthroughs while simultaneously acknowledging the ethical implications of AI advancements. Rigorous testing, transparent development practices, and continuous evaluation become integral components of responsible innovation.

2. Establishing Ethical Guidelines: To guide the development and deployment of AI, America must spearhead the establishment of comprehensive ethical guidelines. These guidelines should address issues such as transparency, accountability, privacy, and fairness. Through

collaborative efforts with experts, policymakers, and global partners, a framework can be created that sets a gold standard for AI ethics.

3. Investing in AI Education and Research: A robust AI strategy necessitates significant investments in education and research. By empowering the workforce with the necessary skills and knowledge, America ensures that its citizens are not only adept users but also contributors to the AI landscape. This investment extends to fostering research institutions that drive innovation and address ethical considerations.

4. Collaboration with Global Partners: AI knows no borders, and its development requires a collaborative approach. America should actively engage with global partners, fostering an open dialogue on AI development, sharing best practices, and collectively addressing challenges. By leading collaborative initiatives, America can contribute to a global consensus on responsible AI use.

5. Nurturing a Culture of Inclusivity: In the pursuit of AI excellence, inclusivity becomes paramount. America's strategy should prioritize the involvement of diverse voices in AI development, ensuring that the technology is representative and caters to the needs of a varied global population. Inclusivity also extends to mitigating biases and prejudices in AI algorithms.

6. Transparency in AI Systems: Transparency is a linchpin in building trust in AI systems. America should advocate for transparent development processes, making it clear how AI algorithms function and the ethical considerations embedded in their design. This transparency empowers users and the broader public to understand and engage with AI technologies.

7. Addressing Privacy and Security Concerns: To safeguard the adoption of AI, America must proactively address privacy and security concerns. Stringent measures should be implemented to protect individuals' privacy while also fortifying AI systems against potential cyber threats. A comprehensive strategy should be devised to strike a delicate balance between innovation and security.

8. Promoting AI for Social Good: America's AI strategy should not only focus on economic gains but also prioritize the use of AI for social good. Initiatives that leverage AI to address societal challenges, enhance healthcare, improve education, and combat climate change can showcase the positive impact of AI on humanity.

9. Continuous Adaptation and Regulation: As AI evolves, America's strategy should embrace continuous adaptation. Regular assessments and updates to ethical guidelines and regulatory frameworks will be crucial. Collaborative efforts with international bodies can contribute to the establishment of global standards, preventing the misuse of AI and ensuring its responsible development.

10. Advocating for a Human-Centric Approach: At the heart of America's AI strategy is a commitment to a human-centric approach. AI should serve humanity, augmenting human capabilities rather than replacing them. By championing a vision where AI aligns with human values and aspirations, America can lead the world toward a future where technology enhances the human experience.

This chapter presents a strategic blueprint for America's leadership in AI development, emphasizing responsible innovation, ethical considerations, global collaboration, and a commitment to a human-centric approach to ensure the best and safest utilization of artificial intelligence.

Chapter 31
The Hydrogen Revolution

America's Transition to a Clean Energy Future

As the world stands at the crossroads of energy transition, hydrogen emerges as the beacon guiding the path to a clean, sustainable future. This chapter delves into the dynamics of the hydrogen revolution, emphasizing the need for determination and clear thinking to propel America into a leadership role. Drawing parallels with the historic adoption of fossil fuels, we explore the transformative potential of hydrogen as the fuel that not only sustains progress but also safeguards the planet.

1. The Evolutionary Spark of Fossil Fuels: Fossil fuels, the catalysts of human evolution, provided the momentum needed for progress and dominance. Acknowledging their pivotal role becomes the first step in appreciating the journey that brought us here. It is time to recognize and appreciate the spark that fossil fuels ignited, propelling humanity forward.

2. Hydrogen - The Clean Energy Carrier: In the quest for a sustainable future, hydrogen emerges as the torchbearer of clean energy. An energy carrier rather than a source, hydrogen holds the promise of harnessing diverse renewable energy sources and converting them into a clean, efficient fuel. Its versatility makes it a cornerstone for a myriad of applications.

3. The Determination to Change Course: As America once harnessed the power of fossil fuels with determination and vision, it stands at the precipice of a new era with hydrogen. The determination to change course and embrace a clean energy future becomes imperative. This shift requires bold decisions, strategic investments, and unwavering commitment.

4. Harnessing Hydrogen for Development: Just as fossil fuels fueled America's development and global dominance, hydrogen has the potential to play a similar role in the Fourth Industrial Revolution. It is not just a fuel but a versatile building block that can power industries, transportation, and energy systems with minimal environmental impact.

5. Leading the Transitional Period: America, with its historical precedent in leading transitional periods, can once again guide the world through the hydrogen revolution. By adopting hydrogen as a primary energy carrier, America can set the standard for transitioning away from fossil fuels, showcasing the potential for sustainable progress.

6. The Clean Energy Imperative: The imperative to embrace clean energy is not just an environmental necessity but a strategic advantage. Hydrogen, as a clean and efficient energy carrier, aligns with America's commitment to environmental stewardship. It positions the nation as a global leader in a paradigm shift towards sustainable energy.

7. Overcoming Hesitation: Transitioning from fossil fuels to hydrogen demands overcoming hesitation and embracing change. Just as the world

hesitated before embracing oil, it now faces a pivotal moment with hydrogen. America's readiness to navigate this uncharted territory will influence global attitudes and accelerate the global adoption of hydrogen.

8. The Strategic Role of Hydrogen: Understanding the strategic role hydrogen can play is pivotal. It is not merely a replacement for fossil fuels but a transformative force driving innovation across sectors. By strategically integrating hydrogen into the national energy landscape, America can ensure energy security, economic resilience, and environmental sustainability.

9. Fostering Global Collaboration: The hydrogen revolution transcends national borders. America's leadership requires fostering global collaboration. Engaging with international partners, sharing expertise, and co-developing hydrogen technologies will amplify the impact and accelerate the global transition to a hydrogen-powered future.

10. Hydrogen - A Catalyst for Progress and Sustainability: In embracing hydrogen, America embraces a catalyst for progress and sustainability. It is a strategic choice that not only ensures energy security but also positions the nation as a steward of the planet. Hydrogen becomes the driving force behind a cleaner, more resilient, and interconnected world.

This chapter illuminates the potential of hydrogen as the fuel of the Fourth Industrial Revolution, urging America to lead the way with determination, clear thinking, and a commitment to a clean energy future.

Chapter 32
The Symbiosis of AI and Hydrogen

Catalysts for a Revolutionized World

In the intricate dance of progress, the convergence of Artificial Intelligence (AI) and Hydrogen emerges as a symphony orchestrating a harmonious future. This chapter explores the transformative synergy between these two technologies, painting a vivid picture of how their coexistence can not only redefine how we live and work but also reignite the global economy, creating a wave of opportunities across countless sectors.

1. The Symbiotic Dance: As AI and Hydrogen join hands, they engage in a symbiotic dance that transcends traditional boundaries. AI's ability to process immense data meets Hydrogen's potential as a clean energy carrier, sparking a revolution that goes beyond mere technological advancement.

2. Catalyzing the Global Economy: Together, AI and Hydrogen become catalysts for economic revitalization. Their integration into various sectors sparks innovation, creating a ripple effect that generates countless jobs and fuels economic growth. This symbiosis sets the stage for a global economic resurgence.

3. Reinventing Transportation: In the realm of transportation, AI and Hydrogen collaborate to reinvent how we move. AI-driven autonomous vehicles powered by hydrogen fuel cells revolutionize public transport, reducing emissions and increasing efficiency. The result is not just a shift in technology but a reimagining of urban mobility and logistics.

4. The Information Superhighway: AI becomes the engine that drives the information superhighway, transforming how we transfer knowledge and communicate. Coupled with the energy efficiency of hydrogen, data centers and communication networks become sustainable, reducing their environmental impact while enhancing connectivity on a global scale.

5. AI and Hydrogen in the Workplace: Workplaces undergo a profound transformation with the integration of AI and Hydrogen. From intelligent automation that enhances productivity to clean energy solutions that power industries, the coexistence of these technologies creates a paradigm shift in how we work. New job opportunities emerge in AI development, renewable energy, and tech-driven industries.

6. Smart Cities and Infrastructure: AI and Hydrogen form the backbone of smart cities, where data-driven decision-making meets clean, sustainable energy. From optimizing energy consumption to managing traffic flows, these technologies revolutionize urban living. The development of smart infrastructure becomes a cornerstone of economic development.

7. Healthcare Revolution: In healthcare, AI becomes a diagnostic powerhouse, analyzing vast datasets to personalize treatments and accelerate medical research. Hydrogen contributes to clean and efficient power solutions for hospitals and medical facilities, ensuring a sustainable healthcare ecosystem.

8. Environmental Stewardship: AI and Hydrogen converge as champions of environmental stewardship. AI algorithms monitor and manage environmental data, while hydrogen powers clean energy solutions, reducing carbon footprints. This synergy fosters a sustainable future, aligning economic growth with ecological responsibility.

9. Agriculture and Food Production: The agricultural landscape undergoes a revolution as AI optimizes farming processes, from precision agriculture to automated harvesting. Hydrogen-powered solutions fuel machinery, offering a clean alternative to traditional farming practices. This transformation creates opportunities across the entire food production chain.

10. Shaping a Better Life: Ultimately, the coexistence of AI and Hydrogen shapes a better life for individuals and communities. It transcends the realms of technology and economy, offering a vision where innovation, sustainability, and economic prosperity harmonize to create a world that is not just advanced but also equitable, inclusive, and environmentally conscious.

This chapter paints a portrait of a future where the symbiosis of AI and Hydrogen becomes a catalyst for positive change, ushering in a new era of innovation, economic growth, and sustainable living.

Chapter 33

"The AI-Hydrogen Symphony at Home"

In the not-so-distant future, the harmonious convergence of Artificial Intelligence (AI) and hydrogen will revolutionize our households. Picture a home where the orchestration of these technological wonders creates a symphony of efficiency, sustainability, and comfort.

Intelligent Energy Management:

Imagine an AI-driven system seamlessly managing your home's energy needs. The refrigerator intuitively adjusts its power consumption based on usage patterns, optimizing efficiency without compromising freshness. The oven, guided by AI algorithms, cooks meals with precision, minimizing energy waste.

Hydrogen-Powered Cooking:

Enter the kitchen of tomorrow, where hydrogen is the fuel of choice. Clean-burning and environmentally friendly, hydrogen gas fuels stovetops and ovens. Say goodbye to traditional cooking methods as hydrogen flames dance elegantly beneath pots and pans, providing instant and controlled heat.

Smart Electricity Supply:

The household of the future operates on an intelligent electricity supply network. AI predicts your energy needs and communicates with hydrogen fuel cells to generate power efficiently. During low-demand periods, excess energy is stored as hydrogen, ready to power your home during peak times or even provide electricity to the grid.

Hydrogen-Powered Heating and Cooling:

Bid farewell to traditional heating and cooling systems. Hydrogen fuel cells efficiently produce electricity and, as a byproduct, generate heat. Your home is warmed in winter without the need for separate heating systems. In the scorching summer, AI ensures your cooling system operates optimally, powered by stored hydrogen energy.

Sustainability at Its Core:

The marriage of AI and hydrogen isn't just about convenience; it's a commitment to sustainability. Hydrogen, a clean energy carrier, releases only water vapor when utilized. AI algorithms constantly analyze and adjust energy consumption, ensuring your home minimizes its carbon footprint.

Customized Comfort:

Picture an AI that learns your preferences. The smart home adapts to your habits, adjusting temperatures, cooking times, and lighting based on your daily routine. The result? Unparalleled comfort tailored to your lifestyle.

Energy Resilience:

AI's predictive capabilities extend to energy resilience. In the event of power outages, your home seamlessly transitions to hydrogen power, ensuring uninterrupted functionality. Your smart appliances continue to operate, offering a glimpse into a future where energy disruptions are relics of the past.

As we stand at the cusp of this AI-Hydrogen era, the household becomes a testament to innovation, sustainability, and a glimpse into a future where technology serves humanity and the planet. Embrace the symphony – your home is now a conductor of the AI-Hydrogen revolution.

Chapter 34

"The Transformative Duo: Hydrogen and AI in the Workplace"

In the coming years, the seamless integration of hydrogen and Artificial Intelligence (AI) will redefine the landscape of work, shaping a future where innovation meets sustainability. Let's explore the profound impact this transformative duo will have on the way we work, the environments we work in, job creation, energy efficiency, and the overall ease that AI promises to bring into our professional lives.

Smart Offices:

The traditional office space will undergo a metamorphosis into intelligent, energy-efficient hubs. AI algorithms will optimize lighting, heating, and cooling systems based on real-time occupancy and usage patterns, creating workspaces that adapt to the needs of employees.

Hydrogen-Powered Industries:

Industries, powered by hydrogen, will witness a revolution. Manufacturing plants, once reliant on conventional energy sources, will adopt hydrogen fuel cells, reducing emissions and energy costs. AI-driven automation will streamline processes, enhancing efficiency and output.

Job Creation in Sustainable Sectors:

The integration of hydrogen and AI will spur job creation in sustainable sectors. New roles will emerge in the development, maintenance, and innovation of AI-driven technologies, as well as in the burgeoning hydrogen industry. The workforce will evolve to meet the demands of a green and technology-centric economy.

Energy Consumption Revolution:

AI's predictive capabilities coupled with hydrogen's clean energy production will revolutionize energy consumption in workplaces. Smart grids will optimize energy distribution, utilizing stored hydrogen during peak demand. This dynamic interplay ensures energy efficiency and cost-effectiveness, reducing the environmental impact of daily operations.

Ease in Daily Work Life:

AI will serve as a digital assistant, enhancing productivity and easing the daily work life of employees. From managing schedules to automating routine tasks, AI allows human workers to focus on creative and strategic aspects of their roles. Hydrogen-powered technologies will ensure a reliable and uninterrupted energy supply for these AI-driven systems.

Sustainable Remote Work:

The rise of remote work will be empowered by sustainable technologies. AI will facilitate seamless communication and collaboration, making virtual work environments more efficient. Hydrogen-powered systems will provide energy resilience for those working remotely, contributing to a sustainable work-from-home model.

Environmental Stewardship in Business:

The integration of hydrogen and AI represents a commitment to environmental stewardship in business. Companies adopting these technologies will position themselves as pioneers in sustainability, appealing to environmentally conscious consumers and contributing to the global shift toward a greener economy.

As we navigate the evolving landscape of work, the marriage of hydrogen and AI emerges as a catalyst for positive change. From sustainable practices and job creation to energy efficiency and streamlined work processes, this transformative duo promises a future where the workplace aligns with the principles of innovation, sustainability, and human-centric design.

Chapter 35

"Revolutionizing Heavy Jobs: AI and Hydrogen in Manual Professions"

In the dynamic world of manual professions like construction, plumbing, and electrical work, the fusion of Artificial Intelligence (AI) and hydrogen technologies is set to bring about a revolutionary transformation. This chapter delves into how these groundbreaking advancements will reshape heavy jobs, ensuring a harmonious synergy between human expertise and cutting-edge technologies.

AI-Assisted Construction:

In the construction industry, AI will serve as a digital assistant, streamlining project management, scheduling, and resource allocation. Builders and contractors will benefit from predictive analytics, optimizing workflows and minimizing delays. AI-driven drones and robots will take on hazardous tasks, enhancing safety on construction sites.

Precision Plumbing with Hydrogen Energy:

Hydrogen fuel cells will power precision tools in plumbing, offering reliable and emission-free energy. Plumbers will experience increased mobility as hydrogen-powered vehicles become commonplace. AI will assist in diagnostics, providing real-time information on potential issues, thus facilitating proactive maintenance and minimizing downtime.

Intelligent Electrical Work:

Electricians will witness a shift toward intelligent electrical systems, where AI monitors and manages energy consumption. Hydrogen-powered backup systems will ensure uninterrupted power supply during outages, critical for maintaining the functionality of electronic tools and equipment.

AI-Driven Safety Protocols:

Safety is paramount in heavy jobs. AI algorithms will analyze and predict potential safety hazards, allowing workers to implement proactive measures. Wearable devices equipped with AI will monitor vital signs, ensuring the well-being of workers in challenging environments.

Automated Heavy Machinery:

Construction equipment and heavy machinery will undergo a paradigm shift with AI automation. From excavators to cranes, these machines will operate more efficiently, reducing the physical strain on operators. Hydrogen fuel cells will replace traditional power sources, minimizing environmental impact.

Skills Enhancement through AI Learning:

AI-driven training modules will empower workers with continuous skills enhancement. Virtual reality (VR) and augmented reality (AR) simulations will create immersive learning experiences for new and seasoned professionals alike, fostering a culture of ongoing education within heavy job industries.

Green Construction Practices:

The integration of hydrogen as a clean energy source aligns with the growing emphasis on green construction practices. Heavy job professionals adopting hydrogen-powered tools and equipment contribute to reducing the carbon footprint of their activities, showcasing a commitment to sustainability.

Hydrogen-Powered Mobile Workstations:

Mobile workstations powered by hydrogen fuel cells will serve as on-site hubs for heavy job professionals. These stations will offer reliable energy for charging tools and devices, creating a portable and sustainable solution for professionals working in diverse locations.

In the realm of heavy jobs, the combination of AI and hydrogen technologies offers a transformative journey toward efficiency, safety, and sustainability. As these innovations become integral to daily operations, professionals in manual professions will navigate a future where cutting-edge technologies complement and elevate their expertise.

Chapter 36

"The Future Road: AI and Hydrogen in Transportation Revolution"

Embarking on the highways of innovation, the transportation sector is set for a monumental transformation through the integration of Artificial Intelligence (AI) and hydrogen technologies. This chapter explores the myriad ways these cutting-edge solutions will revolutionize cars, trucks, airplanes, trains, and even automated vehicles, creating an interconnected and intelligent transportation ecosystem with a focus on safety, efficiency, and environmental sustainability.

Hydrogen-Powered Cars:

The automotive landscape is undergoing a green renaissance with hydrogen-powered cars taking center stage. AI-driven systems optimize fuel efficiency, predict maintenance needs, and enhance safety. Hydrogen fuel cells provide a clean alternative, reducing emissions and fostering a sustainable approach to personal transportation.

AI-Enhanced Traffic Management:

Urban congestion becomes a relic of the past as AI takes the reins of traffic management. Smart algorithms optimize traffic flow, reduce bottlenecks, and predict peak hours. Hydrogen-powered sensors and cameras contribute to efficient road monitoring, ensuring a smooth and safe journey for all.

Autonomous Vehicles:

AI-driven autonomous vehicles are becoming integral to transportation. Hydrogen fuel cells power these vehicles, offering extended ranges and quick refueling. AI algorithms govern navigation, avoiding collisions, and adapting to dynamic traffic conditions, presenting a vision of safer and more reliable autonomous transportation.

Hydrogen-Powered Trucks:

Long-haul trucking sees a green revolution as hydrogen-powered trucks take to the highways. AI-assisted route planning optimizes fuel consumption, while hydrogen fuel cells deliver the torque needed for heavy loads. The result is an eco-friendly and efficient freight transportation system.

Aviation Innovation:

Hydrogen propulsion enters the skies, transforming the aviation industry. AI algorithms manage flight paths, optimize fuel usage, and predict maintenance requirements. Hydrogen-powered airplanes reduce carbon emissions, marking a milestone toward sustainable air travel.

Hydrogen-Fueled Trains:

Traditional train networks experience an eco-friendly makeover with hydrogen-powered trains. AI systems monitor track conditions, optimize schedules, and ensure safety. Hydrogen fuel cells provide a silent and emissions-free alternative for urban and long-distance rail travel.

Automated Public Transportation:

Public transportation becomes more accessible and efficient with automated systems. AI-controlled buses and trains navigate predetermined routes, adapting to passenger demands and traffic conditions. Hydrogen fuel cells contribute to clean energy solutions for mass transit.

Road Safety and Monitoring:

AI-equipped monitoring systems enhance road safety. Cameras, sensors, and drones powered by hydrogen fuel cells ensure real-time surveillance of road conditions. AI algorithms predict potential hazards, allowing for proactive safety measures and minimizing accidents.

Eco-Friendly Infrastructure:

The integration of hydrogen refueling stations along highways complements the widespread adoption of hydrogen-powered vehicles. AI algorithms optimize the placement of these stations, ensuring convenient access for drivers and promoting the growth of a sustainable infrastructure.

The marriage of AI and hydrogen technologies in the transportation sector presents a vision of interconnected and intelligent mobility. From hydrogen-powered cars to AI-driven traffic management, this chapter explores the transformative journey toward a safer, more efficient, and environmentally conscious transportation ecosystem.

Chapter 37

"Empowering Lives: AI and Fuel Cell Synergy for Human Well-Being"

In the tapestry of human existence, the collaborative dance of Artificial Intelligence (AI) and fuel cell technology unfolds as a transformative symphony, orchestrating a myriad of enhancements to human well-being. This chapter explores the profound ways in which the fusion of AI and fuel cell technology contributes to healthcare, life expectancy, and the holistic well-being of individuals across the spectrum of age and experience.

AI-Driven Personalized Healthcare:

AI algorithms, intertwined with fuel cell-powered medical devices, revolutionize healthcare. Personalized treatment plans, diagnosis, and monitoring tailored to individual needs usher in an era of precision medicine, ensuring more effective and targeted healthcare interventions.

Fuel Cell Implants for Lifelong Health:

The marriage of AI and fuel cell technology introduces intelligent implants that continuously adapt and respond to the body's needs. These implants, powered by clean hydrogen energy, enhance physiological functions, providing a fountain of health throughout a person's life.

Pediatric Care Reinvented:

AI-fueled diagnostics and predictive analytics, coupled with hydrogen-powered medical equipment, redefine pediatric care. From early disease detection to tailored treatments, infants and children experience improved healthcare outcomes, setting the stage for healthier lives.

Teenage Well-Being Programs:

AI-driven well-being programs, supported by fuel cell technology, address the unique challenges faced by teenagers. Personalized mental health support, nutritional guidance, and educational interventions ensure a holistic approach to nurturing the well-being of the youth.

Middle-Aged Health Optimization:

Fuel cell-powered wearables seamlessly integrated with AI algorithms assist individuals in maintaining optimal health during their middle years. From fitness monitoring to stress management, these technologies empower individuals to make informed choices for their well-being.

Elderly Care Revolutionized:

AI-enhanced robotics, supported by hydrogen fuel cells, redefine elderly care. Intelligent companions, personalized healthcare assistance, and advanced mobility solutions ensure that the elderly experience dignity, independence, and well-being in their golden years.

Newborn Health Surveillance:

AI-driven monitoring systems, powered by clean fuel cell energy, provide comprehensive surveillance for newborns. Early detection of health issues, coupled with prompt interventions, contributes to improved neonatal health and increased life expectancy.

Nutritional Optimization through AI:

AI algorithms, analyzing individual dietary needs, collaborate with hydrogen-rich nutrition plans. Tailored nutritional recommendations ensure that individuals receive the essential elements for physical and mental well-being, fostering a culture of preventive healthcare.

AI-Powered Psychological Support:

AI-driven mental health applications, supported by sustainable fuel cell energy, become stalwart companions in the pursuit of psychological well-being. These applications offer personalized interventions, therapy, and emotional support, contributing to enhanced mental health for individuals of all ages.

AI for Health Recovery:

AI-driven rehabilitation programs, combined with hydrogen-powered medical equipment, expedite the recovery process after illnesses or surgeries. Adaptive and personalized recovery plans cater to individual needs, optimizing the journey back to health.

In the harmonious interplay of AI and fuel cell technology, humanity finds a harmonious melody of well-being. This chapter celebrates the fusion of innovation and compassion, showcasing how these technologies collaboratively uplift, empower, and enrich the human experience across all stages of life.

Chapter 38

"Educational Renaissance: Fueling Minds with AI and Hydrogen"

Embarking on a transformative journey, the synergy of Fuel Cells and Artificial Intelligence (AI) heralds an educational renaissance, revolutionizing every stage of learning from elementary school to the highest degree. This chapter delves into the profound impact of these technologies on shaping not just knowledgeable individuals, but critical thinkers, innovators, and open-minded contributors to a brighter future.

Elementary Education Envisioned:

Fuel cell-powered smart classrooms, supported by AI-driven adaptive learning systems, create immersive and dynamic environments for young learners. Personalized learning plans cater to individual needs, fostering curiosity, creativity, and a joy for exploration.

Middle School Metamorphosis:

AI algorithms, seamlessly integrated with clean hydrogen energy, facilitate interactive learning experiences in middle schools. These technologies provide students with tools for hands-on experimentation, collaborative projects, and exposure to diverse perspectives, nurturing a holistic understanding of knowledge.

High School's Gateway to Possibilities:

Fuel cell technology powers cutting-edge laboratories and AI-driven educational platforms, amplifying the high school experience. Students engage in real-world problem-solving, critical analysis, and project-based learning, preparing them for the complexities of the future.

University Level Unleashed:

AI-supported lecture platforms, enhanced by hydrogen fuel cells, transform higher education into a dynamic realm of exploration. Virtual labs, interactive simulations, and collaborative research opportunities redefine traditional learning, fostering independent thinking and innovative problem-solving skills.

AI Tutors for Lifelong Learning:

Beyond formal education, AI-driven tutoring platforms, fueled by hydrogen energy, become lifelong learning companions. Individuals of all ages access personalized learning modules, adapting to their evolving interests and ensuring continuous intellectual growth.

Critical Thinking Cultivated:

AI-infused curriculum designs, coupled with fuel cell-powered experiential learning, prioritize critical thinking skills at every educational level. Students are encouraged to question, analyze, and synthesize information, preparing them to navigate an ever-evolving knowledge landscape.

Diversity in Educational Content:

AI algorithms, guided by sustainable hydrogen energy, curate diverse educational content. This ensures that students are exposed to a rich tapestry of perspectives, histories, and ideas, fostering a global mindset and cultural appreciation.

Ethical Decision-Making Education:

AI-driven ethical decision-making modules, supported by clean fuel cell technology, become integral to educational curricula. Students learn to navigate the complexities of moral reasoning, empathy, and responsible use of technology, contributing to a society of ethically conscious individuals.

Hybrid Learning Ecosystems:

Fuel cell-powered educational platforms facilitate seamless hybrid learning experiences. AI-driven assessments gauge individual progress, allowing educators to tailor interventions and support, ensuring that no learner is left behind.

AI-Fueled Educational Innovation:

Continuous advancements in AI, coupled with sustainable fuel cell energy, encourage educational institutions to innovate. Virtual reality classrooms, AI-assisted research, and interdisciplinary learning opportunities redefine the educational landscape, creating a breeding ground for innovation and progress.

In the harmonious marriage of AI and hydrogen fuel cells, education transcends traditional boundaries, empowering minds to think critically, question relentlessly, and contribute meaningfully to the world. This chapter paints a vision of an educational ecosystem where technology is not just a tool but a catalyst for human intellectual and ethical growth.

Chapter 39

"Societal Symphony: Harmonizing Relationships with AI and Fuel Cells"

In the era of Artificial Intelligence (AI) and Fuel Cell Revolution, societal relationships undergo a transformative symphony, influencing family bonds and fostering harmony among nations. This chapter illuminates the myriad ways in which these technologies contribute to a better and more connected world.

Family Dynamics Enhanced:

AI-driven smart home assistants, powered by clean hydrogen energy, create an environment of efficiency and convenience within households. Automated tasks, personalized recommendations, and thoughtful anticipatory actions alleviate stress, allowing families to focus on meaningful connections and shared experiences.

AI Counsel for Relationship Wellness:

Couples and families benefit from AI-powered relationship counselors, ensuring open communication, understanding, and conflict resolution. This digital support, fueled by sustainable hydrogen energy, promotes emotional well-being and strengthens the foundations of familial bonds.

Educational Partnerships for Parents:

AI-assisted educational platforms, integrated with fuel cell technology, provide parents with insights into their children's learning journeys. This collaborative approach fosters stronger parent-teacher relationships, enabling a supportive network for educational development.

Global Diplomacy Enhanced:

AI-driven diplomatic simulations, supported by clean hydrogen energy, offer nations a platform for conflict resolution and negotiation. Virtual forums powered by these technologies facilitate open dialogue, reducing misunderstandings and contributing to peaceful international relations.

Cross-Cultural Understanding:

AI-driven translation tools, harnessing the power of fuel cells, break down language barriers and foster cross-cultural understanding. Individuals from different linguistic backgrounds connect effortlessly, nurturing global friendships and collaborations.

AI-Powered Healthcare Diplomacy:

Collaborative AI-driven healthcare initiatives, sustained by hydrogen technology, promote international cooperation in addressing health crises. Real-time data analysis and resource-sharing contribute to a global healthcare ecosystem that transcends borders.

Sustainable Living Agendas:

AI-supported sustainable living campaigns, empowered by fuel cell advancements, inspire communities and nations to adopt eco-friendly practices. Shared environmental goals foster a sense of collective responsibility and cooperation.

AI-Guided Conflict Resolution:

AI algorithms, powered by clean hydrogen energy, contribute to conflict resolution efforts. Predictive analytics and data-driven strategies assist in identifying root causes and implementing preventive measures, leading to more stable societies.

Virtual Diplomatic Exchanges:

AI-driven virtual diplomatic summits, supported by hydrogen fuel cells, enable leaders to engage in dialogue without geographical constraints. This facilitates more frequent and accessible international collaborations, strengthening global partnerships.

Humanitarian Aid Optimized:

AI-powered logistics, coupled with fuel cell technology, streamline humanitarian efforts. Faster response times, efficient resource allocation, and data-driven decision-making enhance the effectiveness of aid, fostering a sense of global interconnectedness.

In this era of interconnectedness, AI and fuel cell technologies serve as catalysts for societal harmony. By fostering understanding, efficiency, and sustainability, these innovations contribute to a world where relationships are nurtured, and collective well-being becomes a shared responsibility. The symphony of societal connections resonates with the transformative power of AI and fuel cells, harmonizing the intricate melodies of family, community, and global relationships.

Chapter 40

"Democratic Renaissance: Empowering Citizens with AI and Fuel Cells"

In the tapestry of democracy, Artificial Intelligence (AI) and Fuel Cells weave transformative threads, redefining how we collectively shape our future. This chapter explores the ways in which these technologies enhance democratic values, fostering connectivity, informed decision-making, and efficient governance at all levels.

Decentralized Decision-Making:

AI-driven platforms, powered by sustainable hydrogen energy, decentralize decision-making processes. From local town halls to national assemblies, these technologies facilitate more direct citizen participation, ensuring a democratic governance structure that is responsive to diverse needs.

Informed Voting through AI Assistance:

AI algorithms, fueled by clean hydrogen energy, empower voters with comprehensive information about candidates and issues. Personalized voter guides, fact-checking tools, and real-time policy analysis contribute to an informed electorate, enhancing the democratic voting process.

Secure and Transparent Elections:

Blockchain technology, coupled with AI-powered data security protocols, ensures secure and transparent elections. Decentralized ledgers, supported by fuel cell technology, safeguard the integrity of the electoral process, fostering trust in democratic institutions.

AI-Enabled Civic Education:

AI-driven educational platforms, sustained by hydrogen energy, promote civic awareness and engagement. Virtual simulations, interactive learning experiences, and real-world applications of democratic principles prepare citizens to actively participate in shaping their communities.

Smart Governance for Efficient States:

AI-driven governance models, integrated with fuel cell advancements, optimize resource allocation and service delivery. Predictive analytics and data-driven policies enhance the efficiency of state functions, promoting good governance at every administrative level.

Community Feedback Loops:

AI-driven feedback mechanisms, powered by hydrogen energy, enable citizens to provide continuous input on local initiatives. This creates a dynamic feedback loop between government and constituents, ensuring policies align with the evolving needs of communities.

Connectivity of Rural and Urban Grids:

AI-enhanced smart grids, supported by fuel cell technology, bridge the gap between rural and urban communities. Efficient energy distribution and communication networks connect disparate regions, ensuring equal access to resources and opportunities.

Virtual Town Halls and Public Forums:

AI-driven virtual town halls, sustained by clean hydrogen energy, facilitate public discourse and civic engagement. Citizens from small towns to metropolitan areas can participate in meaningful discussions, transcending geographical limitations.

Cross-Border Collaborations:

AI-powered diplomatic forums, empowered by fuel cells, foster international collaborations. Democratic values extend beyond borders as nations engage in open dialogue, sharing experiences and collectively addressing global challenges.

Transparent Government Accountability:

AI-driven analytics, coupled with fuel cell sustainability, enhance government transparency. Citizens have real-time access to information about policy decisions, budget allocations, and the impact of government actions, fostering trust and accountability.

In the nexus of AI and fuel cell advancements, democracy flourishes as a dynamic, inclusive, and responsive system. These technologies democratize information, amplify citizen voices, and create interconnected grids that empower communities at all levels. As we embrace this democratic renaissance, AI and fuel cells become indispensable tools for fostering a future where democratic values thrive and collective decision-making shapes the destiny of nations.

Chapter 41

"Harmony of Artistry: Elevating Creativity with AI and Fuel Cells"

In the realm of artistic expression, the fusion of Artificial Intelligence (AI) and Fuel Cells orchestrates a symphony of innovation, breathing new life into music, poetry, dance, and the entire spectrum of the arts. This chapter explores how these technologies contribute to the flourishing of creativity, providing new avenues for artistic expression and cultivating a renaissance in the world of culture.

AI-Generated Compositions:

AI algorithms, fueled by sustainable hydrogen energy, collaborate with musicians to compose original pieces. This collaboration pushes the boundaries of musical exploration, offering unique melodies and harmonies that blend tradition with avant-garde expression.

Interactive Art Installations:

Fuel cell-powered interactive art installations, guided by AI, create immersive experiences. Sculptures and paintings respond dynamically to viewers, fostering a deeper connection between the audience and the artwork, blurring the lines between observer and creator.

Dance Choreography Innovation:

AI-assisted choreography, energized by clean hydrogen technology, introduces novel dance forms. Dancers collaborate with AI to explore innovative movements and expressions, pushing the boundaries of traditional dance and creating performances that resonate with contemporary audiences.

Poetic Collaborations:

AI-generated poetry, sustained by hydrogen energy, collaborates with human poets to craft verses that evoke deep emotions and explore uncharted linguistic landscapes. This synergy invites poets to experiment with language, bringing forth new narratives and metaphors.

Smart Studios for Visual Arts:

AI-powered studios, supported by fuel cell efficiency, enhance the creative process for visual artists. These studios analyze artistic preferences, recommend techniques, and provide real-time feedback, empowering artists to explore new mediums and styles.

Augmented Reality in Sculpture:

AI-enhanced augmented reality, powered by hydrogen energy, transforms the world of sculpture. Artists can create virtual sculptures that interact with physical spaces, offering viewers a multisensory experience that transcends traditional sculptural limitations.

Collaborative AI-Infused Music Festivals:

Fuel cell-supported music festivals harness the power of AI to curate diverse lineups, ensuring a rich and varied musical experience for attendees. These festivals become collaborative platforms where human and AI-generated music harmonize.

AI-Driven Film and Performance Arts:

AI-driven script analysis and performance optimization, fueled by clean hydrogen, revolutionize filmmaking and live performances. Real-time adjustments based on audience reactions and preferences create dynamic and engaging cinematic experiences.

Digital Art Collectives:

AI-fueled digital art collectives, supported by fuel cell sustainability, connect artists globally. Collaborative platforms enable artists to contribute to shared projects, fostering a sense of community and expanding the reach of artistic expression.

Creative Occupation in a Leisure Society:

As AI and fuel cells reduce the necessity for traditional work, individuals find more time for artistic pursuits. A leisure society emerges, where people can immerse themselves in creative endeavors, contributing to a cultural renaissance.

In the harmonious interplay of AI and fuel cell technologies, the arts evolve into a dynamic force, reflecting the spirit of an ever-changing world. These innovations not only expand the palette of artistic possibilities but also democratize the creative process, inviting individuals from all walks of life to participate in the ongoing cultural evolution. As we witness the emergence of a new era in artistic expression, AI and fuel cells stand as catalysts, enriching our shared cultural tapestry with vibrant hues of creativity.

Chapter 42

"Innovation Unleashed: Transforming the Sporting Arena with AI and Fuel Cells"

In the dynamic world of sports, the integration of Artificial Intelligence (AI) and Fuel Cells unfolds a new era of innovation, redefining how athletes perform, referees officiate, and audiences engage with sporting events. This chapter explores the groundbreaking ways in which these technologies revolutionize various sports, from the grandeur of the Olympic Games to the electrifying energy of football in the Champions League.

AI-Enhanced Athlete Performance:

Fuel cell-powered wearables, synchronized with AI algorithms, provide athletes with real-time insights into their performance. From monitoring vital signs to suggesting personalized training regimens, this collaboration helps athletes reach their peak potential and prevents injuries.

Fair Play and AI Refereeing:

AI-powered referee assistance systems bring an unparalleled level of accuracy to decision-making. Video analysis, supported by hydrogen energy, ensures fair play by minimizing errors, promoting justice on the field, and upholding the spirit of competition.

Fuel Cell-Powered Sports Equipment:

Cutting-edge sports gear, energized by fuel cell technology, enhances durability and performance. From lightweight bicycles to high-speed racing cars, the sports industry embraces sustainable energy solutions, reducing environmental impact and setting new standards for efficiency.

Smart Stadiums:

AI-driven stadium management, powered by fuel cells, transforms the spectator experience. Smart ticketing, personalized concessions, and enhanced security protocols create a seamless and secure environment, amplifying the joy of attending live sporting events.

Augmented Reality for Fan Engagement:

Fuel cell-supported augmented reality applications elevate fan engagement. Spectators can enjoy immersive experiences, such as holographic player introductions and interactive game statistics, enhancing their connection with the sports they love.

AI-Generated Sports Analytics:

AI algorithms, energized by hydrogen, generate comprehensive sports analytics. From player performance metrics to strategic insights, coaches and analysts leverage this data to refine training methodologies and gain a competitive edge.

Hydrogen-Powered Athletic Recovery:

Fuel cell technology supports advanced recovery solutions for athletes. From hydrogen-infused therapies to portable recovery stations, these innovations expedite the healing process, enabling athletes to recuperate faster and maintain peak performance.

Global Accessibility through AI Coaching:

AI-driven coaching platforms, fueled by hydrogen, democratize sports education. Athletes worldwide can access personalized coaching programs, fostering talent development in regions where professional coaching may be limited.

AI-Enhanced Sports Broadcasting:

Fuel cell-supported AI algorithms optimize sports broadcasting. Dynamic camera angles, instant replays, and personalized commentary cater to individual viewer preferences, enhancing the overall experience for audiences.

Energy-Efficient Sports Events:

Hydrogen fuel cells power sports events with minimal environmental impact. From lighting stadiums to supplying energy for ancillary services, these clean energy solutions contribute to sustainable and eco-friendly sporting spectacles.

In this era of AI and fuel cell integration, sports transcend traditional boundaries, embracing innovation that benefits athletes, spectators, and the planet. As these technologies continue to evolve, the world of sports becomes a vibrant arena where excellence, fairness, and sustainability converge, creating a thrilling spectacle for all to enjoy.

Chapter 43

"Accelerating Connectivity: The Synergy of AI, Fuel Cells, and High-Speed Telecommunications"

In the interconnected landscape of the 21st century, the convergence of Artificial Intelligence (AI), Fuel Cells, and high-speed telecommunications has ushered in a new era of unparalleled connectivity. This chapter delves into the transformative impact of these technologies, illustrating how they collectively propel the world towards faster, more efficient, and interconnected realms.

AI-Optimized Telecommunications Networks:

Fuel cell-powered data centers drive the backbone of high-speed telecommunications networks. AI algorithms optimize data routing, ensuring minimal latency and maximizing bandwidth efficiency, thereby enabling instantaneous and seamless global communication.

Hydrogen-Powered 5G Infrastructure:

Fuel cell technology supports the energy demands of 5G infrastructure, a cornerstone for ultra-fast and reliable connectivity. This collaboration results in lower energy consumption, reduced environmental impact, and the ability to support an unprecedented number of connected devices.

Smart Cities and AI-Driven Networks:

AI, fueled by hydrogen energy, orchestrates smart city initiatives. From traffic management to energy distribution, these systems optimize urban living, creating connected environments where information flows effortlessly, promoting efficiency, and enhancing the overall quality of life.

Global Internet Accessibility:

Fuel cell-supported AI technologies work synergistically to address global internet accessibility challenges. Through the deployment of hydrogen-powered satellite networks and AI-driven content delivery systems, even remote regions gain high-speed internet access, bridging digital divides.

AI-Enhanced Cybersecurity:

AI algorithms, supported by hydrogen energy, fortify cybersecurity measures. Advanced threat detection, autonomous response mechanisms, and secure data transmission protocols safeguard the integrity of high-speed telecommunications networks, ensuring privacy and reliability.

Telemedicine and Remote Connectivity:

Fuel cell-powered AI facilitates seamless telemedicine experiences. High-speed connectivity enables real-time remote consultations, AI-assisted diagnostics, and continuous patient monitoring, revolutionizing healthcare accessibility and delivery worldwide.

AI-Driven Content Delivery:

Fuel cell-supported content delivery networks (CDNs) enhance the efficiency of delivering digital content. AI algorithms predict user preferences, optimize streaming quality, and minimize buffering, creating a fluid and personalized online experience for users globally.

Edge Computing for Instantaneous Responses:

Fuel cell-supported edge computing, propelled by AI, reduces latency in telecommunications. By processing data closer to the source, this collaboration enables instantaneous responses, benefitting applications ranging from online gaming to critical infrastructure management.

Sustainable Connectivity:

Hydrogen-powered AI systems contribute to sustainable connectivity solutions. By reducing the carbon footprint of telecommunications infrastructure, this collaboration aligns with global efforts to create environmentally conscious and energy-efficient networks.

AI-Enabled Information Accessibility:

Fuel cell-supported AI applications democratize information accessibility. Through advanced language processing and content summarization, these technologies break down language barriers and ensure that information is universally accessible in real-time.

As AI, Fuel Cells, and high-speed telecommunications intertwine, a world of interconnected possibilities emerges. From rapid information exchange to sustainable connectivity solutions, this triad of technologies shapes a future where global communication is not only instantaneous but also intelligent and sustainable.

Chapter 44

"Green Harvest: AI and Fuel Cells Transforming Agriculture"

In the heart of agriculture, a silent revolution takes root as Artificial Intelligence (AI) and Fuel Cells unite to redefine farming practices. This chapter delves into the ways these technologies converge to create a sustainable, efficient, and environmentally conscious agricultural sector.

Pesticide-Free Precision Farming:

AI-driven drones and sensors, powered by hydrogen fuel cells, revolutionize pest management. Real-time monitoring identifies pests and diseases, enabling targeted interventions and reducing the need for harmful pesticides. This not only safeguards crop health but also promotes eco-friendly farming practices.

Sustainable Energy for Farms:

Fuel cell technology provides a clean and sustainable energy source for farms. By replacing traditional fossil fuels, this innovation minimizes environmental impact and sets the stage for eco-conscious farming, aligning with global sustainability goals.

Smart Irrigation Systems for Water Conservation:

AI algorithms, fueled by hydrogen, optimize irrigation. These systems analyze weather patterns, soil conditions, and crop requirements to ensure efficient water distribution, conserving water resources and fostering sustainable water management.

Quality Enhancement Through AI Grading:

Hydrogen-powered AI grading systems enhance the quality of agricultural products. From fruits to grains, these systems assess size, ripeness, and overall quality, ensuring only premium produce reaches consumers, reducing waste and enhancing freshness.

Efficient Supply Chain Management:

AI applications, supported by fuel cells, optimize the agricultural supply chain. Predictive analytics and real-time data enable efficient distribution, reducing transportation needs and minimizing the carbon footprint associated with food delivery.

Instant Farm-to-Table Delivery:

Hydrogen-powered AI facilitates instant delivery of fresh produce. Through smart refrigeration systems and AI-driven logistics, agricultural products reach households, restaurants, and markets swiftly, preserving nutritional value and flavor.

Reducing Land Use and Enhancing Productivity:

AI-driven precision agriculture, in tandem with fuel cell technology, allows for more efficient land use. By maximizing productivity and reducing waste, these technologies contribute to sustainable agriculture practices, minimizing the expansion of farmlands into natural ecosystems.

Minimizing Agricultural Runoff:

Fuel cell-supported AI assists in managing fertilizers and nutrients. Precision application, guided by AI insights, minimizes agricultural runoff, reducing water pollution and safeguarding aquatic ecosystems.

Pollution-Free Energy for Farming Operations:

Fuel cells provide pollution-free energy for farming machinery. From tractors to harvesters, this innovation reduces the environmental impact of traditional petrol-based equipment, contributing to cleaner air and healthier ecosystems.

Eco-Friendly Crop Breeding:

AI, supported by hydrogen, accelerates sustainable crop breeding. Genetic analysis and breeding simulations enable the development of crops resilient to climate change, reducing the need for chemical inputs and enhancing overall agricultural sustainability.

In this eco-conscious revolution, AI and Fuel Cells emerge as stewards of sustainable agriculture, offering a vision where innovation nurtures the land while meeting the growing demands of a hungry world. As these technologies intertwine, they sow the seeds of a greener harvest, ensuring a future where agriculture and ecology thrive in harmony.

Chapter 45

"Beyond Fields: AI and Fuel Cells Transform Onshore and Offshore Agriculture"

Venturing beyond traditional farmlands, the integration of Artificial Intelligence (AI) and Fuel Cells heralds a new era in onshore and offshore agriculture. This chapter explores how these technologies revolutionize agricultural practices, promoting sustainable and humane methods of production.

Optimized Animal Husbandry:

AI-driven monitoring systems, powered by hydrogen fuel cells, redefine animal farming. Real-time data analytics help in creating personalized nutrition plans for livestock, ensuring optimal health without relying on excessive hormones or antibiotics. This approach aims to enhance animal well-being and reduce the environmental impact of conventional practices.

Precision Fish Farming:

Offshore aquaculture undergoes a transformation with AI and Fuel Cells. Automated feeding systems, monitored by AI algorithms, ensure precise nutrition for fish, reducing overfeeding and minimizing environmental pollution. Hydrogen-powered energy sources support offshore fish farms, providing a sustainable alternative to conventional energy supplies.

Reducing Chemical Dependency:

Both onshore and offshore, AI-driven sensors detect early signs of diseases in animals and aquatic life. This early detection minimizes the need for extensive use of pesticides and antibiotics, promoting a healthier environment and reducing the risk of antibiotic resistance.

Enhanced Animal Welfare:

AI applications, fueled by hydrogen, contribute to enhanced animal welfare. Smart monitoring systems ensure that animals are raised in humane conditions, with AI algorithms assessing and responding to their needs. This approach aims to reduce stress and improve the overall quality of animal products.

Efficient Feed Production:

AI-driven optimization of feed production, coupled with hydrogen-powered processing facilities, results in more efficient and sustainable animal nutrition. This process focuses on reducing waste, enhancing nutrient absorption, and minimizing the ecological footprint associated with feed production.

Eco-Friendly Wool Production:

AI-supported breeding programs, powered by hydrogen, enable the development of healthier sheep breeds for wool production. By focusing on genetic traits that promote wool quality, farmers can reduce the reliance on chemicals and produce high-quality wool in an environmentally conscious manner.

Smart Transportation and Distribution:

AI-driven logistics, supported by hydrogen fuel cells, revolutionize the transportation and distribution of animal products. From temperature-controlled storage to optimized routes, these technologies ensure that dairy, meat, and other products reach consumers in a timely and fresh manner, reducing waste and improving overall efficiency.

Aquaponics for Sustainable Yield:

AI-managed aquaponics systems, powered by fuel cells, integrate fish farming with plant cultivation. The symbiotic relationship between fish and plants creates a closed-loop system where fish waste provides nutrients for plants, and plants help filter and clean the water. This approach maximizes resource use efficiency and minimizes environmental impact.

Offshore Renewable Energy for Agriculture:

Fuel cell technology facilitates the integration of renewable energy sources offshore. Wind and solar energy, harnessed by hydrogen fuel cells, power onshore and offshore agricultural operations, reducing dependence on fossil fuels and contributing to sustainable energy practices.

In this realm where land meets sea, AI and Fuel Cells emerge as guardians of responsible agriculture, reshaping how we raise and cultivate animals while prioritizing environmental sustainability and animal welfare. This synergy between technology and ecology paves the way for a more harmonious coexistence between humans and the diverse life forms that share our planet.

Chapter 46

"Smart Cities, Clean Futures: AI and Fuel Cells in Urban Cleaning"

In the bustling urban landscapes of the future, Artificial Intelligence (AI) and Fuel Cell technologies converge to redefine the approach to city cleanliness. This chapter delves into the transformative potential of automated cleaning systems, driven by the analytical power of AI and the sustainable energy provided by Fuel Cells.

Intelligent Waste Management:

AI algorithms, integrated with Fuel Cell-powered sensors, enable real-time monitoring of waste levels in bins and containers across the city. Smart waste management systems optimize collection routes, reducing fuel consumption and emissions while ensuring timely and efficient removal of waste.

Automated Street Sweeping:

Fuel Cell-driven street sweeping vehicles, guided by AI navigation systems, autonomously clean urban streets. These intelligent machines analyze patterns of foot traffic, vehicular movement, and weather conditions to optimize cleaning schedules. The result is a cleaner and more aesthetically pleasing urban environment.

Robotic Public Spaces Cleaning:

AI-enabled robotic devices, powered by hydrogen fuel cells, autonomously navigate public spaces, such as parks and squares, to collect litter and maintain cleanliness. These robots adapt to dynamic environments, responding to human activities and events, ensuring a consistently clean and welcoming atmosphere.

Efficient Graffiti Removal:

AI-driven surveillance cameras, coupled with hydrogen-powered graffiti removal systems, detect and analyze instances of vandalism in real time. Automated cleaning drones equipped with Fuel Cells respond swiftly to remove graffiti, maintaining the visual appeal of public spaces.

Smart Waterway Cleaning:

Fuel Cell-powered autonomous boats equipped with AI-driven sensors monitor and clean urban waterways. These intelligent vessels identify and collect debris, contributing to pollution prevention and maintaining the ecological balance of urban aquatic environments.

Air Quality Improvement:

Hydrogen fuel cells support mobile air purifiers guided by AI algorithms that analyze air quality data. These devices move through urban areas, identifying pollution hotspots and actively purifying the air, contributing to improved respiratory health for city dwellers.

Data-Driven Park Maintenance:

AI-driven analysis of park usage patterns informs predictive maintenance of green spaces. Fuel Cell-powered landscaping equipment ensures timely mowing, pruning, and irrigation, enhancing the aesthetic appeal and recreational value of urban parks.

Eco-Friendly Public Restroom Management:

AI-powered sensors in public restrooms, coupled with hydrogen fuel cells, enable intelligent water usage and waste management. These systems ensure the efficient operation of facilities while minimizing water waste and maintaining hygiene standards.

Noise Pollution Control:

AI-powered noise monitoring devices, supported by hydrogen fuel cells, analyze urban soundscapes. Automated systems respond to excessive noise levels, implementing measures such as sound barriers or scheduling construction activities during non-peak hours to mitigate noise pollution.

Green Building Maintenance:

Fuel Cell-powered drones equipped with AI-driven cameras inspect and clean the exteriors of tall buildings. This proactive approach ensures the longevity of infrastructure while preserving the visual appeal of the cityscape.

In the synergy between AI and Fuel Cells, cities transform into self-regulating entities, dynamically adapting to the needs of their residents. The marriage of intelligence and sustainability propels urban environments toward a future where cleanliness is not just a goal but an inherent characteristic, fostering a higher quality of life for all.

Chapter 47

"From Prevention to Empowerment: AI and Fuel Cells Against Crime"

This chapter explores the transformative potential of Artificial Intelligence (AI) and Fuel Cell technologies in the fight against crime, recognizing that true change begins with addressing the root causes that lead individuals toward criminal activities.

Youth Empowerment Initiatives:

Leveraging AI-driven career counseling platforms, youth in underserved communities can explore a plethora of opportunities tailored to their interests and skills. Fuel Cell-backed educational grants and scholarships ensure that financial constraints don't hinder their pursuit of knowledge.

Accessible Quality Education:

AI-driven personalized learning systems, powered by sustainable Fuel Cells, revolutionize education. Virtual classrooms, adaptive learning modules, and free educational resources enable individuals, regardless of their socio-economic background, to access quality education.

Healthcare Outreach and Mental Well-being:

AI-powered health monitoring, coupled with hydrogen fuel cell support for mobile clinics, ensures that communities receive timely medical attention. Mental health initiatives, guided by AI algorithms, identify individuals at risk and provide proactive support.

AI-Assisted Job Placement:

Advanced AI algorithms match individuals with job opportunities based on their skills, interests, and local demand. Fuel Cell-sponsored vocational training programs equip them with the skills needed for sustainable employment.

Community Policing Reinvented:

AI-driven predictive policing models, backed by sustainable energy sources, focus on preventing crime rather than reactive responses. Smart surveillance, community engagement through AI interfaces, and innovative patrolling strategies build trust and ensure safety.

Social Reintegration Programs:

AI-powered analytics assess the unique needs of individuals reintegrating into society after incarceration. Support programs, coupled with Fuel Cell-backed vocational training, create a supportive environment for successful reintegration, reducing recidivism.

Economic Opportunities Through AI Startups:

Fuel Cell-supported grants and incentives foster the growth of AI startups addressing societal challenges. These startups create jobs, encourage innovation, and contribute to economic development, providing alternatives for individuals tempted by criminal activities.

AI for Conflict Resolution:

AI-powered mediation platforms offer alternative dispute resolution mechanisms. These technologies, supported by sustainable energy, provide fair and unbiased conflict resolution, reducing instances of violence and crime arising from disputes.

Community-Based Rehabilitation Centers:

Fuel Cell technology ensures the sustainability of community-based rehabilitation centers. AI-driven counseling and skill-building programs within these centers empower individuals to break free from cycles of criminal behavior.

Global Collaboration Against Human Trafficking:

AI algorithms, fueled by sustainable energy, analyze vast datasets to identify patterns indicative of human trafficking. International cooperation, facilitated by AI, enables swift responses to combat this heinous crime and support victims.

By addressing the root causes of criminal behavior and empowering individuals with education, healthcare, and economic opportunities, the combined force of AI and Fuel Cells becomes a formidable weapon against crime. The goal is not just to punish but to prevent, rehabilitate, and create a society where everyone has the chance to flourish.

Chapter 48
Capitalizing on Progress

An Open Letter to Visionary Investors

Dear Visionary Investors,

In the corridors of power and influence, where decisions shape the destiny of nations, we stand at a pivotal juncture. The convergence of Artificial Intelligence (AI) and Hydrogen beckons, not merely as technological advancements but as catalysts for a future where prosperity, innovation, and sustainability intertwine. This letter is an appeal, an acknowledgment, and a call to action.

1. Recognizing the Power of Capital: Capital has long been the driving force behind progress. Today, it holds the key to unleashing the full potential of AI and Hydrogen, technologies poised to redefine our world. Your ability to harness capital is not just an opportunity; it is a responsibility to shape a future where economic prosperity aligns seamlessly with environmental stewardship.

2. A Better Tomorrow Through Risk-Taking: Risk-taking has been the heartbeat of every great venture. Embracing the potential of AI and Hydrogen demands a departure from the familiar, a willingness to venture

into uncharted territory. Your capacity to take calculated risks can fuel an unprecedented era of innovation, job creation, and economic growth.

3. Investing in Sustainable Progress: As stewards of capital, investing in sustainable progress is not just a choice; it is an imperative. AI and Hydrogen offer the promise of clean energy, job creation, and technological leadership. By directing investments towards these transformative technologies, you contribute not only to the success of your enterprises but to the well-being of humanity.

4. A Legacy of Innovation and Leadership: The legacy you leave is not solely defined by financial gain but by the impact your investments make on the world. Investing in AI and Hydrogen positions you as pioneers in a new age of innovation and leadership. It is an opportunity to shape history and be remembered as architects of a better future.

5. Overcoming Fear with Courage: Fear often accompanies monumental decisions. However, courage is the force that transcends fear. Embrace the courage to invest in AI and Hydrogen, knowing that your actions today will reverberate through generations. The courage to lead in times of uncertainty sets the stage for triumphs that echo in the annals of history.

6. A Gift to Future Generations: Your contribution to the AI and Hydrogen revolution is not merely an investment; it is a gift to future generations. By fostering innovation, creating sustainable solutions, and

advancing technologies that transcend current limitations, you lay the foundation for a world where prosperity and progress coexist harmoniously.

7. International Acclaim and Leadership: Investing in AI and Hydrogen propels not just your enterprises but the nation and the world forward. It establishes you and the nation as global leaders in a transformative era. The international community will recognize and applaud the visionaries who champion progress, sustainability, and innovation.

8. A Call to Collaboration: The challenges we face demand collaborative efforts. Engage with fellow visionaries, industry leaders, and policymakers. Collaborate to create an environment where AI and Hydrogen can flourish, fostering a global ecosystem that transcends borders for the collective benefit of humanity.

9. A Vision for a Better World: Your investments in AI and Hydrogen contribute to a vision of a better world—a world where economic prosperity is intertwined with environmental responsibility, where innovation flourishes, and where the American empire stands as a beacon of progress and leadership.

In concluding, your visionary investments in AI and Hydrogen are not just a financial endeavor; they are a commitment to a future where the American empire leads with courage, innovation, and sustainability. Your actions today shape the legacy of tomorrow, a legacy that transcends profit margins to become a gift to humanity.

With unwavering belief in progress,a visionary and free spirit

Chapter 49

Unleashing Brilliance

A Strategic Call for Global Talent Adoption

In the grand narrative of history, nations ascend to greatness by embracing the brilliance of minds worldwide. America, with its rich legacy of diversity, stands at the threshold of a transformative strategy to harness global talent. This chapter outlines a visionary approach, urging the nation to cast aside racial discrimination, welcome foreign talent, and in doing so, showcase a unique form of American strength — recognizing the superiority of others.

1. Embracing the Global Tapestry: At the heart of this strategy lies a profound recognition of the immeasurable value that global talent brings. Let us embrace the world as a reservoir of diverse brilliance, recognizing that tapping into this wealth of knowledge can fuel innovation, economic growth, and societal progress.

2. A Bold and Open Invitation: Initiate an unreserved, open invitation to the world's brightest minds. Declare America's commitment to embracing talent without reservations. In demonstrating an open society that welcomes individuals regardless of origin, we create a dynamic ecosystem where ideas flourish, and diverse perspectives drive progress.

3. Reimagining Immigration Policies: Revise immigration policies to dismantle barriers that hinder the entry of skilled individuals, entrepreneurs, scientists, and artists. Seek a balance that ensures national security without compromising the enrichment of American society through global talent.

4. Innovation Hubs as Melting Pots: Establish designated innovation hubs that serve as melting pots for global talent. These hubs should not only facilitate creativity, collaboration, and entrepreneurship but also embody a commitment to inclusivity. They become spaces where excellence knows no borders.

5. Global Collaboration with Educational Institutions: Forge robust partnerships with renowned educational and research institutions worldwide. Facilitate exchange programs and collaborations that bring the best minds to America's shores. By fostering a global network of talent, America ensures a continuous influx of expertise that propels us forward.

6. Investment in Knowledge and Research: Channel substantial resources into education and research. Foster an environment where students and researchers from around the world are drawn to American institutions. By investing in cutting-edge research and providing world-class education, America becomes a beacon for knowledge seekers worldwide.

7. Nurturing Startups and Entrepreneurship: Create initiatives and incentives that support startups and entrepreneurship, acknowledging that

groundbreaking ideas can come from every corner of the globe. By nurturing the entrepreneurial spirit of global talent, America sets the stage for innovation that transcends boundaries.

8. Championing Inclusivity and Diversity: Champion inclusivity and diversity as fundamental values. Establish programs that celebrate and support a multicultural society. Let us embrace different perspectives, cultures, and ideas, fostering an environment where innovation thrives amidst a tapestry of backgrounds.

9. Public Awareness and Advocacy: Launch a comprehensive public awareness campaign that underscores the importance of global talent. Counteract negative narratives by sharing success stories that highlight the immense contributions immigrants have made throughout history. Advocate for policies that reflect America's commitment to being a global talent magnet.

10. Building a Legacy Through Recognition: View this strategy as an investment in the legacy America leaves for future generations. By recognizing the talent and superiority of others, we redefine strength. The renaissance sparked by the adoption of global talent will define the nation's trajectory, showcasing a legacy of innovation, progress, and sustained excellence.

In embracing a strategy that attracts the best and brightest from around the world, America lays the groundwork for a renaissance that transcends racial divides. Let our strength be in recognizing the superiority of others, for in doing so, we build a nation where excellence knows no borders.

Chapter 50

The Open Heart of America

Embracing Diversity as a Pillar of Strength

In the grand tapestry of nations, one thread uniquely weaves through the very fabric of America — an open society that stands as a testament to the nation's resilience, innovation, and unparalleled success. As we navigate the intricate journey of American identity, this chapter celebrates the richness of our open society, a mosaic of diverse talents that has been, and continues to be, the cornerstone of our triumphs.

1. The Essence of America's Open Society: At the heart of America's exceptionalism lies its open society — a welcoming embrace that transcends borders and welcomes the world's aspirations. This openness is not just a characteristic; it's the essence that has fueled our journey from inception to global prominence.

2. A Nation Built on Immigrants: From the shores of Ellis Island to the bustling metropolises of today, America has been and continues to be a magnet for dreamers and doers worldwide. Our foundations are deeply rooted in the stories of those who sought refuge, opportunity, and a chance to contribute to the American dream.

3. A Mosaic of Cultures and Talents: Imagine America as a grand mosaic, each piece representing a different culture, background, and story. It is this diversity that has painted our nation with vibrant hues, creating a dynamic and resilient tapestry that evolves with every new chapter of immigration.

4. Fueling Economic Prosperity: Our open society has not only fostered a sense of unity but has also been a driving force behind economic prosperity. Waves of immigrants have brought their unique skills, work ethic, and entrepreneurial spirit, contributing to the economic engine that propels America forward.

5. The Spirit of Innovation: Innovation thrives in an environment where diverse perspectives collide. From Silicon Valley to research labs, the amalgamation of talents from every corner of the globe has led to groundbreaking inventions and transformative ideas that have reshaped industries and defined eras.

6. The Heartbeat of American Culture: Our culture, a living entity, pulsates with the rhythms of myriad traditions. From cuisine to music, literature to art, the fusion of diverse cultural expressions has created an American identity that is ever-evolving and beautifully complex.

7. Embracing Change and Evolution: An open society does not fear change; it welcomes it. The ability to adapt and evolve, absorbing the

influences of new cultures and perspectives, has been the secret sauce behind America's resilience and continuous reinvention.

8. A Beacon of Freedom and Opportunity: Our open society serves as a beacon, radiating the ideals of freedom and opportunity to the world. It stands as a testament to the American belief that anyone, regardless of their origins, can carve out a path to success and contribute to the nation's narrative.

9. The Responsibility of Sustaining Openness: As we celebrate the beauty of our open society, we must also recognize the responsibility it carries. Sustaining this openness requires an unwavering commitment to inclusivity, fairness, and the acknowledgment that our strength lies in our diversity.

10. A Call to Uphold the American Promise: In the chapters that unfold in the story of America, let us commit to upholding the promise of an open society. For in doing so, we not only honor the legacy of those who came before us but also pave the way for a future where the American mosaic continues to shine bright.

The open heart of America beats with the rhythm of diversity, a melody that resonates with the dreams of all who seek refuge, opportunity, and a chance to contribute to the ongoing symphony of the American experience.

Chapter 51
Lessons from the Shadows

Confronting America's Past Mistakes with Courage

The journey of a nation, much like the odyssey of an individual, is not without its shadows. America, in its storied history, has encountered moments of moral turbulence, lapses in judgment, and actions that, in hindsight, bear the weight of regret. In this chapter, we face these shadows head-on, acknowledging past mistakes, offering self-criticism, and extending a hand in pursuit of understanding and forgiveness.

1. The Native American Tragedy: In the relentless march of westward expansion, America's Indigenous peoples bore the brunt of a tragic tale. The displacement, mistreatment, and dispossession of Native Americans stand as a dark chapter, one that demands acknowledgment, remorse, and a commitment to rectifying historical injustices.

2. Slavery and the Legacy of Racism: The stain of slavery, woven into the fabric of early America, remains a painful scar on the nation's soul. The repercussions of this dark era echo through centuries in the form of systemic racism. We confront the ghosts of our past, recognizing that the journey to equality demands both introspection and systemic change.

3. Japanese Internment during World War II: In the crucible of World War II, fear and prejudice led to the internment of Japanese Americans. This grave injustice, born out of wartime hysteria, teaches us that even in times of crisis, the preservation of civil liberties must be sacrosanct. We reflect on this moment with the humility to learn and vow never to repeat such mistakes.

4. The Tragedy of Vietnam: Thc Vietnam War stands as a somber reminder of the human cost of ideological entanglements. The loss of lives and the enduring scars, both physical and emotional, compel us to question the motivations that led us into this quagmire. Through introspection, we glean insights to guide future decisions.

5. The War on Drugs and Mass Incarceration: The War on Drugs, embarked upon with good intentions, spiraled into a cycle of mass incarceration disproportionately affecting marginalized communities. It is a stark reminder that policies, however well-intentioned, must be critically assessed for their unintended consequences. We seek to rectify the injustices born of these policies.

6. Environmental Exploitation and Neglect: The pursuit of progress has often come at the expense of our environment. From industrial pollution to the exploitation of natural resources, America's footprint on the planet bears marks of shortsightedness. We confront this reality with a commitment to sustainable practices and environmental stewardship.

7. Invasion of Iraq: The invasion of Iraq, rooted in flawed intelligence and geopolitical miscalculations, unfolded as a painful episode. We acknowledge the toll it took on lives and international relations, understanding the imperative of robust checks and balances to prevent such misadventures in the future.

8. Systemic Failures in Healthcare: The shortcomings in America's healthcare system, starkly highlighted by moments of crisis, reveal systemic failures that impact lives. Through critical self-reflection, we confront the need for equitable, accessible healthcare as a fundamental right, not a privilege.

9. The Opioid Crisis: The opioid crisis, fueled by a convergence of factors, illustrates the dangers of unbridled pharmaceutical practices and inadequate regulation. With a commitment to public health, we strive to rectify the mistakes that led to this devastating epidemic.

10. A Pledge to Learn and Grow: In acknowledging these mistakes, we do not dwell in guilt but look forward with a pledge to learn, grow, and foster a nation that continuously evolves. America's resilience lies not in denial but in the courage to face its shadows, emerging stronger with a collective commitment to justice, equality, and a better future.

11. The use of atomic bombs on Hiroshima and Nagasaki by the United States during World War II was a deeply consequential decision, with ethical debates persisting to this day. While proponents argue it hastened

Japan's surrender and potentially saved lives, critics emphasize the immense human suffering and argue that alternative options should have been explored. Additionally, some view it as a demonstration of the newly acquired nuclear power, intended to signal strength to other global powers, a move that sparked profound moral and geopolitical discussions about the use of such devastating weapons.

As we navigate the intricate terrain of our past, let us remember that the journey of self-discovery is ongoing. By confronting our mistakes, we pave a path toward a more enlightened, compassionate, and just America.

Chapter 52
The Subtle Hand of Influence

Navigating the Intersection of Corporations and Education

In the intricate dance between corporations and education, a delicate balance teeters on the precipice of influence. Multinationals, wielding considerable financial power, often find their way into the hallowed halls of academia, influencing not just minds but the very fabric of knowledge dissemination. This chapter delves into the complex relationship between corporations and education, exploring both the positive contributions and the potential pitfalls that demand our vigilance.

1. The Dual Nature of Corporate Influence: Multinationals, with their financial prowess, have played pivotal roles in propelling technological advancements, medical breakthroughs, and economic growth. However, their influence extends beyond innovation, seeping into educational realms where profit motives can clash with the pursuit of unbiased knowledge.

2. The Pharmaceutical Industry and Academic Research: The symbiotic relationship between pharmaceutical giants and academic research is undeniable. While collaborations have led to groundbreaking medical discoveries, the potential for bias in research outcomes and the prioritization of profit over public health demands critical examination.

3. Food Industry and Nutritional Science: In the realm of nutrition, the food industry's influence on academic research has raised questions about the integrity of nutritional science. Conflicting interests may skew findings, affecting public perceptions and policy decisions related to health and dietary guidelines.

4. Fossil Fuel Industry and Environmental Education: The fossil fuel industry, a cornerstone of modern economics, has shaped educational narratives around energy. Yet, questions arise about the potential manipulation of environmental education to downplay the industry's ecological impact. Striking a balance between progress and sustainability becomes paramount.

5. The Dangers of Corporate-Backed Lobbying: Corporate lobbying infiltrates educational policies, influencing curricula and shaping public opinion. The consequences can be profound, potentially steering educational priorities away from holistic learning and critical thinking towards profit-centric perspectives.

6. Lessons from History: Examining historical instances where corporate influence distorted educational narratives provides valuable lessons. From the tobacco industry's denial of health risks to the sugar industry's manipulation of nutritional science, understanding past mistakes is crucial to preventing future pitfalls.

7. The Need for Transparent Partnerships: Transparent collaborations between corporations and educational institutions are essential. Openness about funding sources, research objectives, and potential conflicts of interest safeguards the integrity of academic pursuits and fosters a learning environment free from undue influence.

8. Empowering Educators and Students: Educators, as stewards of knowledge, must navigate the delicate balance between corporate influence and academic integrity. Equipping students with critical thinking skills and an awareness of potential biases ensures they become discerning learners capable of scrutinizing information.

9. The Role of Regulation and Oversight: Governmental bodies and educational institutions should establish robust regulations and oversight mechanisms to mitigate undue corporate influence. By fostering an environment of accountability, we create a safeguard against potential ethical lapses.

10. A Call for Informed Consumerism: In an age where information is abundant, cultivating a population capable of discerning fact from influence is imperative. Promoting media literacy and encouraging informed consumerism empowers individuals to make choices that align with their values and well-being.

11. A Vision for an Educated Future: As we navigate the confluence of corporations and education, envisioning a future where knowledge serves

the greater good is paramount. By learning from past missteps, fostering transparency, and prioritizing critical thinking, we pave the way for an educational landscape that advances societal well-being.

In the evolving dance between corporate interests and the pursuit of knowledge, our collective responsibility lies in preserving the sanctity of education as a force for enlightenment and societal progress.

Chapter 53

Unraveling the Tapestry

Provocative Questions for the Thoughtful Reader

In the labyrinth of existence, we often find ourselves entangled in the narratives we weave — stories of nations, borders, and the grand tapestry of identity. As we navigate this introspective journey, let us pose questions that challenge the very fabric of our beliefs, inviting the reader to explore the essence of existence and the stories we construct.

1. The Fiction of Borders: What if the lines we draw on maps are but figments of collective imagination? Can the reader envision a world where the notion of borders dissolves, and the earth becomes a shared home for all, unrestricted by the stories of nations?

2. Genes or Dreams: Do our genes define us more than our aspirations and dreams? Can we liberate ourselves from the predetermined narratives of superiority based on genetic predispositions and embrace the boundless potential of human endeavor?

3. The Anthem of Humanity: If the world had one anthem, not tied to nations but resonating with the shared human experience, what would it sound like? Can the reader envision a melody that transcends borders, echoing the unity of humanity?

4. The Myth of National Superiority: What if the concept of national superiority is but a myth, a story told to fortify identities? Can we, as readers, question these narratives and recognize the common threads that bind us as inhabitants of a shared planet?

5. Flags as Symbols or Shackles: Are flags symbols of unity, or do they inadvertently become shackles that confine us to prescribed identities? Can the reader envision a world where the colors of flags represent shared aspirations rather than divisive allegiances?

6. The Recyclable Organism: In contemplating life as a recyclable organism, can the reader embrace the freedom that comes with the absence of a predetermined purpose? What if the absence of a specific goal allows us to craft our own destinies and seek meaning on our terms?

7. Imaginary Constructs of Nationhood: What if the reader were to deconstruct the narratives of nationhood, recognizing them as stories woven to instill a sense of belonging? Can we envision a reality where identity transcends prescribed constructs, fostering unity rather than division?

8. Beyond the Earthly Horizon: If we lift our gaze beyond the constraints of earthly perspectives, can the reader imagine a universe indifferent to our narratives of nationhood? What if our shared human experience extends beyond borders, reaching towards the cosmos?

9. The Liberating Power of Self-Reflection: What if self-reflection becomes a powerful tool, enabling the reader to dismantle preconceived notions and explore the limitless possibilities that exist beyond the confines of societal narratives?

10. Crafting Our Own Stories: In embracing the idea that life offers the freedom to create our own goals, can the reader become the author of their narrative, unbound by predetermined scripts? What stories can we craft that redefine our understanding of purpose and meaning?

11. A Journey of Introspection: As the reader engages with these questions, can we embark on a journey of introspection, challenging the stories that shape our perceptions and envisioning a reality where the power to define purpose lies within each individual?

In the quest to unravel the tapestry of existence, these questions serve as threads of inquiry, encouraging readers to question, reflect, and envision a world unburdened by the limitations of predetermined narratives.

Chapter 54
Sharpening the Mind

Igniting Patriotic Inquiry

In the crucible of inquiry, the mind becomes a potent tool for transformation. As we pose questions that challenge the status quo, we embark on a journey of patriotic introspection — not confined to the borders of a single nation but stretching across the tapestry of humanity. This chapter is a call to arms, an invitation to sharpen the mind and engage in a dynamic, patriotic work that transcends boundaries.

1. Beyond National Borders: How can questioning the constructs of borders and identities lead to a broader, more inclusive patriotism that extends beyond the confines of a single nation?

2. The Unity of Human Experience: In envisioning a shared human anthem and recognizing our common threads, how might this foster a sense of global patriotism that unites us in our diversity?

3. Flags as Symbols of Unity: If flags become symbols of shared aspirations rather than divisive allegiances, how can this shift ignite a form of patriotism that embraces collective progress over territorial exclusivity?

4. The Power of Deconstruction: By deconstructing narratives of superiority and dismantling preconceived notions, how can individuals

contribute to a more egalitarian and just form of patriotism that serves humanity as a whole?

5. Crafting Personal Narratives: When individuals become authors of their own stories, liberated from predetermined scripts, how might this contribute to a dynamic patriotism rooted in personal responsibility and meaningful contributions to society?

6. A Universe Beyond Borders: As we lift our gaze towards the cosmos, contemplating a universe indifferent to our earthly narratives, how might this cosmic perspective inform a patriotism that transcends the limitations of our planet?

7. Self-Reflection as a Catalyst: In considering self-reflection as a tool for dismantling societal narratives, how can individuals harness this power to contribute to a patriotic ethos grounded in critical thinking and informed decision-making?

8. A Benevolent Virus of Generosity: As generous ideas spread like a benevolent virus, how can individuals, armed with sharpened minds, become carriers of positive change that influences not only their nation but radiates outward to uplift humanity as a whole?

9. The Dynamics of Development: How does a realistically grounded, dynamic patriotism contribute to national development and innovation,

creating a ripple effect that influences the trajectory of societies on a global scale?

10. Humanity's Collective Journey: What if the journey of patriotic inquiry becomes a collective endeavor, where individuals worldwide contribute to a shared narrative of progress, unity, and prosperity for all?

11. Embracing Realistic Idealism: Can individuals embrace a form of realistic idealism, where the pursuit of noble ideals is anchored in a practical understanding of the world, fostering a patriotism that thrives on pragmatic solutions and inclusive collaboration?

As we delve into these questions, let us collectively sharpen our minds, igniting a patriotic flame that transcends boundaries and propels humanity towards a future characterized by unity, generosity, and shared progress.

Chapter 55

Nurturing the Seeds of Progress

Transformative Investments in Education

In the grand tapestry of a nation's development, education stands as the loom weaving the threads of progress and innovation. This chapter delves into the critical role of education in the cultivation of human resources and explores a transformative vision for educational reform. Drawing inspiration from successful pedagogic models in Scandinavia, Singapore, Switzerland, Israel, and beyond, we explore the profound impact of strategic investments in the youth, setting the stage for a prosperous and enlightened future.

1. The Seeds of Tomorrow: Understanding that the youth are the seeds of tomorrow, how can a nation invest strategically in educational systems that nurture the potential of each individual, fostering a sense of purpose and responsibility?

2. Multi-Dimensional Education: How can the American state envision a multi-dimensional educational process that goes beyond traditional paradigms, embracing holistic development and preparing students not just for careers, but for active citizenship and meaningful lives?

3. The Scandinavian Paradigm: Examining the Scandinavian model, renowned for its emphasis on creativity, critical thinking, and equality, how might the United States draw inspiration to create an educational system that empowers students regardless of socio-economic backgrounds?

4. The Singaporean Blueprint: Considering the success of Singapore's education system, which focuses on academic excellence and practical skills, how can the American educational landscape incorporate similar elements to equip students with a competitive edge in the global arena?

5. The Swiss Approach: Exploring Switzerland's apprenticeship system, recognized for seamlessly integrating education with practical work experience, how can the United States develop vocational training programs that cater to diverse skill sets and bridge the gap between academia and industry?

6. Israeli Innovations: In the context of Israel's innovative education initiatives, how can the United States adapt strategies that encourage entrepreneurship, critical thinking, and technological literacy, laying the groundwork for a future-ready workforce?

7. Quality Over Quantity: Shifting the focus from sheer enrollment numbers to the quality of education, how can the American state prioritize high-quality, accessible education that ensures a deep understanding of core subjects and fosters a lifelong love of learning?

8. Pedagogic Foundations: What are the foundational principles that underpin successful pedagogic systems, and how can these principles be incorporated into the American educational framework to cultivate an environment conducive to intellectual curiosity, creativity, and collaboration?

9. Fostering Responsibility: In instilling a sense of responsibility towards younger generations, how can the American society, including parents, educators, and policymakers, collectively contribute to the success of educational reforms and create a culture that values and supports the journey of learning?

10. Sustainable Investments: Recognizing education as an investment in the nation's future, how can the American state commit to sustainable funding and resource allocation to ensure the continuity and success of educational reforms, laying the foundation for a thriving and innovative society?

11. A Vision for Tomorrow: As we envision the transformative impact of educational reform, how can the United States emerge as a global leader in shaping not just skilled professionals, but compassionate, critically thinking citizens who contribute meaningfully to the advancement of humanity?

This chapter is a call to action, urging the United States to prioritize the education of its youth, drawing inspiration from successful models while embracing innovation to carve a unique path towards a brighter, knowledge-driven future.

Chapter 56
Foundations of Thriving

Nurturing Physical and Mental Well-Being

In the mosaic of societal progress, the individual serves as the cornerstone. This chapter explores the profound interplay between physical and mental health, underscoring the pivotal role each person plays in the collective advancement of society. Delving into the philosophy of holistic well-being, it challenges readers to embark on a journey of self-discovery, understanding that a healthy society burgeons from the wellness of its individuals.

1. The Ripple Effect: How does the well-being of each individual create a ripple effect, influencing the broader tapestry of society?

2. Mind-Body Harmony: In understanding the inseparable connection between physical and mental health, how can individuals cultivate a harmonious relationship between their bodies and minds to navigate the challenges of modern life?

3. The Philosophy of Movement: What role does exercise play in the philosophy of a thriving life, and how can incorporating physical activity become a cornerstone for personal and societal resilience?

4. Exercise as a Ritual: Shifting the perspective of exercise from a mere routine to a sacred ritual, how can individuals infuse intention and mindfulness into their physical activities, transforming them into moments of self-discovery and empowerment?

5. The Shortness of Life: Contemplating the brevity of life, how does the awareness of its fleeting nature inspire individuals to seize each moment with courage, purpose, and an insatiable appetite for personal and collcctive growth?

6. Embracing Challenges: How can the philosophy of embracing challenges and stepping out of one's comfort zone contribute to the development of resilience and mental fortitude, essential components for thriving in a rapidly evolving society?

7. The Courage to Give 100%: Encouraging individuals to give their all, how does the courage to invest 100% of one's existence lead to a sense of fulfillment, purpose, and a positive impact on the world around them?

8. Love of Self and Others: Contemplating the aphorism "love your neighbor as yourself," how can individuals foster a genuine love for others if they have not first cultivated a deep and abiding love for themselves, recognizing the interconnectedness of personal and collective well-being?

9. A Symphony of Wellness: In envisioning a society as a symphony of wellness, how can each individual contribute their unique notes, creating a harmonious melody that resonates across communities and nations?

10. Lifelong Learning and Adaptation: How does the philosophy of continuous learning and adaptation enhance an individual's ability to navigate the complexities of life, fostering a spirit of curiosity and resilience that transcends generational and societal shifts?

11. Cultivating a Thriving Nation: As individuals embark on the journey of self-discovery and well-being, how can this collective pursuit create the fertile ground from which a thriving nation emerges, characterized by innovation, compassion, and sustained growth?

This chapter serves as a poignant reminder that the journey towards a thriving society commences within each person. By prioritizing physical and mental well-being, individuals become architects of a healthier, more vibrant nation.

Chapter 57
The Enigmatic Nature of Man

A Steward for Global Evolution

In the vast menagerie of Earth, the creature known as man stands out not for its speed or strength, but for a unique blend of intellect, adaptability, and an unparalleled ability to shape the course of the world. This chapter delves into the extraordinary qualities of humanity, particularly embodied by the American ideal, and calls for a collective understanding and utilization of these powers for the benefit of all living organisms.

1. The Magical Essence of Man: Exploring the mystical qualities that set humanity apart, how has this remarkable creature, not the fastest or strongest, conquered every corner of the planet, demonstrating an innate ability to influence the destiny of both itself and the broader tapestry of life?

2. A Steward for Global Welfare: Recognizing the unique position of humanity as a steward for the welfare of the planet, how can the collective powers of individuals be harnessed for the greater good, ensuring the prosperity and development of all living organisms?

3. The Power to Shape the Future: Contemplating the inherent ability of mankind to shape its own destiny, how can this power be wielded

responsibly to ensure a future marked by progress, compassion, and symbiosis with the natural world?

4. The American Ideal: Why does the narrative focus on the American ideal? Acknowledging the unparalleled openness and warmth of America in embracing diversity, how does this nation hold a unique position to lead in fostering the broad development of humanity?

5. A Melting Pot of Cultures: Reflecting on the cultural tapestry of America as a melting pot, how has the nation's receptivity to foreigners and diverse ideas contributed to its potential to play a pivotal role in the evolution of global societies?

6. A Love Letter to America: Through the act of expressing love for America, how does this testament signify a shared responsibility to preserve the beauty of this culture for the greater good of humanity, transcending individual identities?

7. A Contribution to Cultural Preservation: In considering the rich American culture as a collective heritage, how can individuals, regardless of origin, play a role in safeguarding the values that make America a beacon of hope and progress?

8. The Beauty of Openness: Celebrating the openness of America, how can this quality be considered a guiding light, illuminating a path toward

unity, understanding, and a shared commitment to the advancement of all living organisms, fostering a global sense of interconnectedness?

9. Embracing the American Ideal: In concluding this chapter, how can the call be extended to individuals worldwide to embrace the American ideal not as a singular national concept, but as a universal aspiration for openness, progress, and global well-being, fostering a collective responsibility for the evolution of humanity?

This chapter serves as a testament to the potential of humanity, embodied in the American ideal, to lead the way in fostering an evolution that transcends borders, embraces diversity, and ensures the prosperity of all living beings.

Chapter 58

Celebrating the Human Tapestry

A Global Mosaic of Beauty

In the vast expanse of Earth, humanity emerges as a wondrous blend of intellect, adaptability, and an extraordinary ability to shape the world. This chapter delves into the exceptional qualities of humanity, epitomized by the diverse tapestry found in the United States, to showcase the universal beauty of human ideals.

1. The Multifaceted Essence of Humanity: Exploring the captivating qualities that set humanity apart, how has this remarkable species, regardless of speed or strength, permeated every corner of the planet, displaying an innate capability to influence its destiny and that of the broader tapestry of life?

2. A Global Steward for Universal Welfare: Recognizing humanity's unique role as stewards for the welfare of the planet, how can the collective powers of individuals be harnessed globally for the greater good, ensuring the prosperity and development of all living organisms?

3. The Power to Shape a Shared Future: Contemplating mankind's inherent ability to shape its destiny, how can this power be wielded

responsibly on a global scale to ensure a future marked by progress, compassion, and symbiosis with the natural world?

4. Embracing the Global Ideal: Rather than focusing on any specific national ideal, how can the narrative celebrate the universality of ideals found within the mosaic of humanity, exemplified by the rich diversity of the United States?

5. A Melting Pot of Cultures on a Global Scale: Reflecting on the worldwide cultural mosaic, how can the receptivity to diversity and the blending of ideas contribute to fostering a global society that transcends borders, religions, and political ideologies?

6. A Love Letter to Humanity: Through an expression of love for the human experience, how does this testament signify a shared responsibility to preserve the beauty of diverse cultures for the greater good of all, transcending individual identities?

7. A Contribution to Global Cultural Preservation: In considering the rich tapestry of global cultures as a collective heritage, how can individuals worldwide play a role in safeguarding the values that make humanity a beacon of hope and progress?

8. The Beauty of Openness on a Global Scale: Celebrating the global openness to diversity, how can this quality be considered a guiding light, illuminating a path toward unity, understanding, and a shared commitment

to the advancement of all living organisms, fostering a global sense of interconnectedness?

9. Embracing the Universal Ideal: In concluding this chapter, how can the call be extended to individuals globally to embrace the universal ideal not as a singular national concept, but as a global aspiration for openness, progress, and the well-being of all, fostering a collective responsibility for the evolution of humanity?

This chapter serves as a testament to the potential of humanity, found within the diverse global mosaic, to lead the way in fostering an evolution that transcends borders, embraces diversity, and ensures the prosperity of all living beings.

In the embrace of the Stars and Stripes, I find my heart dancing to the rhythm of the American dream, a dream woven from the threads of diversity, an unparalleled mosaic of cultures, music, art, and technological wonders. This book, a humble offering, is an ode to the potential embedded within the very soul of the United States of America — a potential that can spark a renaissance, a revival of ideals and dreams.

As I pen down these thoughts, I feel compelled to trace the lines of history, to caution against the repetition of errors that have cast shadows over other empires. Mistakes that, if left unchecked, could unravel the fabric of this magnificent civilization. This literary endeavor is a call for unity, transcending political divides that threaten the harmonious melody of this nation. The current discord among political factions, if exacerbated, may become the discordant note that leads to a symphony's demise.

In contemplating the global stage, I see the need for a recalibration of foreign policies, especially in the face of burgeoning powers like China. The choices made now carry implications not just for the United States but for the very essence of life on our shared planet. Wisdom, I implore, should guide our hands in navigating the complexities that lie ahead.

This book is not merely a collection of words but a humble contribution to reignite the dwindling flame of the American dream. A dream that, for centuries, has been a beacon of hope, radiating far beyond borders. It is a living reality, attainable not by mere wishful thinking but by those with an insatiable hunger for toil, for life, for love, for creation, and for evolution.

Let these pages serve as a testament to our collective responsibility in preserving and nurturing the dreams that have fueled the American spirit. As the ink dries, let it symbolize not an end but a new beginning, a chapter where realistic optimism prevails, and the American dream, rekindled, continues to illuminate the path to a brighter future.

'to be continued'

www.ingramcontent.com/pod-product-compliance
Lightning Source LLC
Chambersburg PA
CBHW071721130725
29531CB00035B/1625
* 9 7 8 1 9 1 7 0 9 5 8 6 0 *